TIFFANY BUCKNER

Soul Ties & Demons

DELIVERANCE

FROM UNGODLY & DEMONIC SOUL TIES

Soul Ties & Demons
by Tiffany Buckner

©2025, Tiffany Buckner
info@anointedfire.com

Published by Anointed Fire™ House
www.anointedfirehouse.com
Cover Design by Anointed Fire

ISBN: 978-1-955557-60-3

TABLE OF CONTENTS

INTRODUCTION

> For the word of God is living and active, sharper than any two-edged sword, piercing to the division of soul and of spirit, of joints and of marrow, and discerning the thoughts and intentions of the heart.
> Hebrews 4:12

There are different types of soul ties, different strengths of soul ties, and different dimensions of soul ties. What's shocking is the fact that most believers have been blinded by the enemy as it relates to the makeup of their souls as well as the overall topic of soul ties. The reason for this is—Satan needs us to remain ignorant if he's going to be successful in his attempts to bind our souls, steal our destinies, and lead us astray. This is why knowledge, while necessary, is not enough. The Bible tells us to also pursue understanding, and this is where the average Christian drops the ball. We like to echo what the Bible says without understanding God's heart behind His Word.

Please note that Satan ensnares us in two dimensions:

☐ Body	☐ Soul

And by "us," I mean believers. Satan cannot bind the spirit of a believer since we are filled with God's Holy Spirit, therefore the enemy of our souls has to set traps for our souls as well as our bodies. By doing this, he can cause us to repeatedly wound ourselves spiritually (see Proverbs 18:14). Below are two scriptural examples:

➤ **1 Corinthians 6:16 (ESV):** Or do you not know that he who is joined to a prostitute becomes one body with her? For, as it is written, "The two will become one flesh."

➤ **Proverbs 22:24-25 (ESV):** Make no friendship with an angry man; and with a furious man thou shalt not go: Lest thou learn his ways, and get a snare to thy soul.

The objective of ungodly soul ties is to:
1. Lock you in a season.
2. Lock you in a cycle.
3. Lock you in a mindset.

By doing this, Satan can control what you see, what you experience, what you feel, and these, in turn, influence what you do. This allows him to steal your faith, getting you to put faith in yourself and in the spirit of this world, rather than placing your faith in the Most High God. This is why this book is so needed in today's Christian climate because, get this, there are more believers who believe the lies of Satan than there are who believe the Word of God. This is to say that soul ties aren't just designed to bind you to a person, their main purpose is to lock you out of God's will for you.

In this groundbreaking, monumental, and incredibly informative book, you will get an ind-depth lesson on the topic of ungodly soul ties and how demons use them to ensnare God's people. You will also learn how to break free and stay free!

Souls & Soul Ties

And it came to pass, when he had made an end of speaking unto Saul, that the soul of Jonathan was knit with the soul of David, and Jonathan loved him as his own soul.

1 Samuel 18:1

There is an ongoing debate in the religious community regarding soul ties. It's not uncommon to hear people say that soul ties aren't real. It's also not uncommon to hear people say, "Show me that in the Bible." Of course, many leaders, including myself, tend to point people to 1 Samuel 18:1, where it says that the soul of Jonathan was knit to the soul of David, but to someone who is committed to their own beliefs, even this scripture isn't enough to prove the validity of soul ties. So, let's start here. What does the word "knit" mean? Merriam Webster's online dictionary defines the word "knit" this way:

1. To form by interlacing yarn or thread in a series of connected loops with needles.
2. To link firmly or closely.

3. To cause to grow together.

What are some synonyms for the word "knit?" According to Thesaurus.com, they are:

bind	crochet	fasten
mend	sew	unite
weave	affiliate	affix
ally	cable	connect
contract	heal	interlace
intermingle	join	link
loop	net	purl
repair	secure	tie

Notice here that the word "tie" is the last word. This is to say that the Bible did and does refer to soul ties; it just doesn't use the actual term "soul tie." All the same, the following scriptures are also referencing soul ties:

- **Genesis 2:24:** Therefore shall a man leave his father and his mother, and shall *cleave* unto his wife: and they shall be one flesh.

- **1 Corinthians 6:15-16:** Know ye not that your

2

bodies are the members of Christ? Shall I then take the members of Christ, and make them the members of an harlot? God forbid. What? Know ye not that he which is joined to an harlot is one body? For two, saith he, shall be one flesh.

- **Genesis 34:2-3:** And when Shechem the son of Hamor the Hivite, prince of the country, saw her, he took her, and lay with her, and defiled her. And his soul *clave* unto Dinah the daughter of Jacob, and he loved the damsel, and spake kindly unto the damsel.

The soul is comprised of the mind, will, and emotions. The mind, biblically speaking, is the heart. This is what God told us to guard. "Keep thy heart with all diligence; for out of it are the issues of life" (Proverbs 4:23). Let's look at the etymology of the word "issue."

c. 1300, "an exit," from Old French issue "a way out, a going out, exit; final event," from fem. past participle of issir "to go out," from Latin exire "go out, go forth; become public; flow, gush, pour forth" (source also of Italian uscire, Catalan exir), from ex- "out" (see ex-) +

ire "to go," from PIE root *ei- "to go."

Meaning "discharge of blood or other fluid from the body" is from 1520s; sense of "offspring, children" is from late 14c. Meaning "outcome of an action, consequence, result" is attested from late 14c., probably from this sense in French. Meaning "action of sending into publication or circulation" is from 1833.

Source: etymonline.com (issue) n.

When God told us to guard our hearts, this suggests that something will make *multiple* attempts to enter our hearts. If it gains access, it then exits or flows from our hearts; therefore, if we are contaminated with lies, we will contaminate the people around us and the people who partake in what we share—people who've opened their hearts to us. This is how false religions, cults, witchcraft movements, and every demonic organization forms. It starts with an individual who has a heart that has been accessed or breached by the enemy. That person became a "patient zero" of sorts or, better yet, a carrier of that diseased doctrine. So, to protect us from becoming carriers of demonic doctrines, God told us to guard our hearts; this way, we wouldn't end up soul-tied to demonic people and compromised souls. This is to say that a soul tie, in layman's terms, is a binding agreement between two souls, after all, "Can two walk together, except they be agreed (see Amos 3:3)? This agreement could be a verbal declaration that you've made in a moment of passion, confusion, or fear; for example, stating that you will be with that person forever. And while we, as humans, tend to say things that we don't mean at times, in the realm of the spirit, everything we say or have said becomes an agreement between us and the people we've made promises to. This is what binds two souls together; this is what we refer to as our bonds with other people.

What is a bond? According to Oxford Languages, a bond is:

Noun:

1. a relationship between people or groups based on shared feelings, interests, or experiences.
2. a connection between two surfaces or objects that have been joined together, especially by means of an adhesive substance, heat, or pressure.

Law:

1. an agreement with legal force.
2. a deed by which a person is committed to make payment to another.

Understand this—while we don't pull out contracts when forming relationships with people, we do form legal agreements with our words. This is why Proverbs 6:2 states, "Thou art snared with the words of thy mouth, thou art taken with the words of thy mouth." Other scriptures to keep in mind include:

- **Matthew 12:36-37:** But I say unto you, That every idle word that men shall speak, they shall give account thereof in the day of judgment. For by thy words thou shalt be justified, and by thy words thou shalt be condemned.
- **Proverbs 18:21:** Death and life are in the power of the tongue: and they that love it shall eat the fruit thereof.
- **2 Timothy 2:16:** But shun profane and vain babblings: for they will increase unto more ungodliness.

A soul tie is as it sounds—a tie, a connection, an

Souls & Soul Ties

agreement between two souls. I share this because we
have spiritualized the concept of having soul ties, and as
a result of this, many people think that soul ties are like
spiritual umbilical cords that can be cut through a soul
tie breaking ceremony. And while you can (and should)
renounce ungodly soul ties, the truth is, agreements go
far deeper than declarations we've made about one
another and promises we've made to one another. We
connect to principles and we connect in principles.
Plainly put, if I start a rally to promote pro-life, I'll
likely meet like-minded people at that rally and I may
connect with a few of those people. If I connected with a
woman named Jennifer, for example, and she had a
change of heart as it relates to pro-life, our connection
would break because we are no longer in agreement—at
least in that section of our souls. We may have formed
other agreements over time, for example, we may both
be activists against kill shelters, which would mean that
we'd still run into one another from time to time, and we
still have an agreement in place. This agreement, while
not necessarily a binding agreement as it relates to laws
and legalities, would still connect us. So, while we may
no longer agree about the rights of unborn children, we

still have an agreement in place. Why is this important? Because a lot of believers today are bound to ungodly soul ties through their ungodly practices. For example, I had a woman to reach out to me once, and I can remember that she was incredibly upset. She wanted me to pray a soul tie breaking prayer, because according to the woman, her ex had moved on with his life, and she was tired of being tortured emotionally. She wanted to move on too. I remember feeling agitated, not so much at her, but at the fact that we have a generation today that thinks that they can cancel the laws of sowing and reaping when what they've reaped mirrors what they've sown. I asked her a simple question. "Did you sleep with him?" She paused before answering. "Yes, I did," she said. In that moment, I had to choose between sparing her feelings and playing into her belief that she was a victim or telling her a truth that could possibly render me as an enemy in her mind. I chose the latter because hell hurts far worse than hurt feelings. I let her know that:

- She'd reaped what she'd sown, after all, if you're not faithful to God, you will reap an unfaithful partner.

- Whoever you present your body to, that is your lord. Jesus said in Luke 6:46, "And why call ye me, Lord, Lord, and do not the things which I say?"

- The pain was not in place to punish her, it was there to warn her of a greater pain. It's like telling your kids not to touch a hot oven, but then pretending not to see them when they choose to do so anyway. The logic behind this is—a first degree burn may save them from eventually getting a bunch of third degree burns.

- She couldn't sever a soul tie as an act of revenge against the devil who'd lied to her. It was almost like saying, "Since you didn't give me what you promised, I'm breaking this soul tie so that I too can be disconnected and emotionally removed from the situation." You can't use God to punish a devil that you're in agreement with; you can't use our Lord and Savior to teach Satan a much-needed lesson, hoping that he'll honor his lies the next time you decide to sin against God in an attempt to get what the devil promised you. It's like being an addict and calling the cops on a drug dealer because you ordered five crack rocks, but the dealer gave you four instead.

- As long as you're in fornication, the agreement still stands because the agreement isn't between you and the ex; the agreement is between you and the enemy of your soul. Your ex simply met you at the same altar because he or she signed that same agreement, and the two of you consummated that agreement when you chose to lie down together.

Now, I didn't say all this to the young lady, but I did say most of it, I'm sure. Thankfully, she wasn't offended because my goal wasn't to judge her, attack her, or make her feel worse than she already felt. My goal was to help her understand that there was no soul tie breaking ritual that could be performed by anybody because soul ties aren't invisible threads that connect us to one another. She needed to change her mind; she needed to come out of agreement with fornication and everything that led her there; this is how the soul tie would be severed. The moment she changed her mind, her perspective, beliefs, and principles would change, which would lead her to a different conclusion. A conclusion ends a season; it is a period at the end of whatever we've sentenced ourselves to.

This is to say that the soul is not a tangible entity that we can touch, reshape, or snatch away from people whenever they prove themselves to be untrustworthy. The soul is the life of a man. Note: the Hebrew word for "soul" is "nephesh," and according to the Lexicon, it means: "life, self, person, heart, creature, mind, living being." Genesis 2:7 introduces us to this principle; it reads, "And the LORD God formed man of the dust of the ground, and breathed into his nostrils the breath of life; and man became a living soul." So then, what exactly is a soul, and how does it differ from the spirit of a man? Your spirit is God's declaration of you; your spirit was formed with God's spoken Word. You are a (lower case) word of God, while Jesus is the (uppercase) Word of God. As a matter of fact, Adam and Eve weren't created in Genesis 3; they were created in Genesis 1. "And God said, Let us make man in our image, after our likeness: and let them have dominion over the fish of the sea, and over the fowl of the air, and over the cattle, and over all the earth, and over every creeping thing that creepeth upon the earth. So God created man in his own image, in the image of God created he him; male and female created he them. And God blessed them, and God said unto them, Be fruitful, and multiply, and replenish the earth, and subdue it: and have dominion over the fish of the sea, and over the fowl of the air, and over every living thing that moveth upon the earth" (Genesis 1:26-28). This was the moment that marked the creation of man, however, in Genesis 3, God formed the body or earth-suit that man was to wear to legalize his existence in the material realm. Genesis 2:6-7 details the formation of man's body and soul; it reads, "But there went up a mist from the earth, and watered the whole face of the ground. And the LORD God formed man of the dust of the ground, and breathed into his nostrils the breath of life; and man became a living soul." You see, our spirit connects us with God, but our soul connects us with our humanity. Therefore, we are hybrids of sorts—spirits/eternal creatures who were made in the image of God, but also souls, creatures who possess the ability to think, feel, and make decisions independent of God and independent of one another in the Earth. This is why we are (lowercase) gods. Knowing this, Satan made his way into the Garden of Eden and introduced Eve to a part of her own technology that she had yet to explore in depth—her will. And within her will was the ability to make a choice that was contrary to what God commanded her. But within each choice is a nucleus. Oxford Languages defines the word "nucleus" as, "the central and most important part of an object, movement, or group, forming the basis for its activity and growth." This is what we call decision. The word "decision" comes from the word "decide," and it has everything to do with the side you take when presented with two or more options. The decision you make then determines the state you find yourself in. In the natural, we can choose to live in California, Alabama, Texas, Michigan, Washington, New York, or whichever state we want to live in. In the supernatural, the choices we make set the stage for the state of mind that we find ourselves in.

Each state has a shape. Let's think naturally again. Texas is shaped like a boot, Michigan is shaped like a mitten, and Ohio is shaped like a toilet bowl. Now, when we talk about mental states, please understand that your mind (not brain) is shaped by agreements. Our minds are shaped by the principles we have and the agreements we've made. This is why some people are in a great state of mind, while others are said to be in bad states, but it's not so much about the states of mind we're in as it is about the templates (principles) that we've allowed to shape our minds. You see, the shape your mind is in will determine the realms you exist in, and your realm will determine your reality. This is the nature of the soul. Your soul ties are a collection of relationships you've formed in the states you're in; this has everything to do with the principles you've come into alignment with and the people you've met while honoring those principles. This is why, in order to break a soul tie, you have to change your mind by changing your state of mind. In other words, you need new information, after all:

1. God formed you.
2. Sin deformed you.
3. The world conformed you to its principles.
4. You have to be transformed by the renewing of your mind.
5. Your mind is renewed through right information. This is what leads to transformation.

All of this has everything to do with your form or the shape of your soul, and your soul is shaped by the information you've welcomed into your heart through agreement.

In this book, you will get a broader understanding of what a soul tie is versus what it is not, as well as how to sever them, break through demonic strongholds, and destroy demonic agreements.

STRONG DELUSION

> And with all deceivableness of unrighteousness in them that perish; because they received not the love of the truth, that they might be saved. And for this cause God shall send them strong delusion, that they should believe a lie: That they all might be damned who believed not the truth, but had pleasure in unrighteousness.
> 2 Thessalonians 2:10-12

You are a spirit living in a body that has a soul. Your body legalizes your existence here on Earth. Anything that lives on Earth must be clothed in an earth-suit unless otherwise permitted by God. So yes, you have angels that are assigned to you. The kingdom of darkness tries to replicate this by assigning demonic spirits to you. Some of the demons assigned to you fall under the category of familiar spirits, and they don't live outside of you; they typically find their abode in you or they'll use the people around you. Spirits can and do enter into objects as well, but they have little to no power there, so they prefer to live in human bodies. Please note that if a demon can't get in you, it'll get around you. In other words, it will infect someone in your immediate circle to gain access to you; that's if it is assigned to you. It will also try to use someone it already has access to, and it will try to pair the two of you up. Where do you think the infamous "type" comes from? For example, when the Philistines could not get to or overtake Samson, they hired Delilah to get them the entail they needed to take Samson down. When Pharaoh wanted to kill off the newborn Israelite males, he commanded the midwives to do his dirty deed. This is simply a warfare tactic, and it's not reserved just for the kingdom of darkness. When God wanted to take down Ahab, He put a lying spirit in the mouths of Jezebel's prophets. When God wanted to protect His people, He placed Joseph in Pharaoh's castle as Pharaoh's right-hand man. And then, there's Esther who found herself married to a pagan king, Daniel who found himself serving as a chief ruler, prophet, and governor in Babylon. There are many tactics used in natural warfare as well as spiritual warfare, and none of these weapons are new. This means that, as a believer, you can effectively learn to fight back against the enemy by simply learning God's Word, the history of warfare, and how certain demons operate.

But first, can a Christian have a demon? This question has been asked by many, but answered by the one and true living God, YAHWEH. He answered this question plainly in the story told in Matthew 15:22-26, which reads, "And, behold, a woman of Canaan came out of the same coasts, and cried unto him, saying, Have mercy on me, O Lord, thou son of David; my daughter is grievously vexed with a devil. But he answered her not a word. And his disciples came and besought him, saying, Send her away; for she crieth after us. But he answered and said, I am not sent but unto the lost sheep of the house of Israel. Then came she and worshiped him, saying, Lord, help me. But he answered and said, It is not meet to take the children's bread, and to cast it to dogs."

The children's bread. Who was Jesus talking about? God's children, of course—you, me, and everyone who has confessed Jesus Christ as their Lord and Savior. So, if deliverance is the children's bread, this means that it is only reserved for believers. It is a rite of passage and a benefit of being a child of God. So yes, Christians can have demons, but here's the thing—we can't be possessed by the devil; we can only be oppressed by him. Possession takes place in the spirit of a person, but oppression takes place in the body and soul.

The soul is comprised of the mind, will, and emotions, and get this, demons can't take over the will of a believer. As a minister of deliverance, I have stood in front of people who were strongly manifesting demons during deliverance while they were behaving violently—thrashing around, growling, pushing their bodies up against mine, and in a few cases, I've had people to start swinging their arms and kicking their feet. But here's the thing. They were not possessed—not if they were believers. What's happening in these moments is—they are receiving demonic imaginations; they are envisioning themselves being violent, and because they are used to giving into temptation, they give into the temptation to be violent. In other words, they are weak-willed. Now, I won't say that this is true for every single soul; I will say that it's true for more than 90 percent of deliverance cases. Once I realized this, I started setting the tone before deliverance, especially in mass deliverance settings, letting the people know that if they start swinging, biting, kicking, and attempting to body slam the people who are ministering deliverance to them—THAT'S NOT THE DEMON MAKING THEM DO THAT! I let them know that they are simply being tempted by those demons, and if they start behaving violently, it is their choice to do so. Get this—when I warn people upfront, they behave and it becomes easier to distinguish the demonic personality from their own, but if I don't give the warning, I know I'll likely have to restrain someone's arms while I'm taking them through deliverance. So now, I am definitely a fan of setting precedence before deliverance takes place; this way, the process can be smooth for the both of us, as well as any other minister who will be ministering deliverance at the event.

What do devils have to do with soul ties and delusion? Absolutely nothing and everything at the same time! Let me explain. A person who is free of demonic bondage can choose to do wrong, just as a person who is bound by a legion of demons can choose to do right. One thing the enemy cannot rob a believer of is his or her ability to choose. After all, demons don't enter people and cause them to make bad choices. Demons come in because the people in question are already making bad choices. This is how the agreements were forged in the first place. For example, the Bible tells us to cast down imaginations and every high thing that exalts itself against the knowledge of God ..." There's a reason for this. A lot of the thoughts we have are not our own. They are demonic commercials playing in our minds designed to seduce us into sin or scare us away from progressing in the faith. This is why God told us to cast them down. If they aren't cast down, they will keep playing until we give into them, or until we get used to them. This is to say that if there is a thought tormenting you, arrest the thought. How do you do this? By taking the Word and piercing the thought with the Word. For example, let's say that your thought-life is often interrupted whenever you are talking to a guy at your local assembly. It would seem as if every time he speaks to you, looks at you, or comes within 50 feet of you, you hear in your mind, "That's your husband." What should you do? First, understand that Satan loves to lead believers into one-sided soul ties so he can tempt them into witchcraft and lead them into delusion. How does this work? It's a common story. A woman sees a man at her church, and she believes that God told her that the guy in question is her God-appointed husband. What's worse is every time she sees the guy, he smiles at her, flirts with her (or so she thinks), and says something that makes her believe that he knows she's his future wife. Let's say that the person he's enticing is you. For example, one Sunday, he'd said to you, "I was helping out in the children's daycare this morning, and those kids are out of line!" He then chuckles before saying, "That's why I don't want no more than three children, maybe four if my wife is up for the challenge! How about you? How many children do you want?" You smile shyly, silently reminding yourself not to break eye contact. "Maybe two or three," you say before looking down at the floor, realizing that you can only maintain eye contact for five seconds before you start behaving awkwardly. "That's good," he says, lowering his voice and his head so that his eyes can meet your eyes once again. "I think you'll make a great mother someday." With those words, he turns around to see who's calling his name. "Oh, gotta go," he says, with his ordinarily elevated tone returning to its normal pitch. "They want me to go back and help with the children. Pray for me! I think the Lord is preparing me for my next season—marriage and fatherhood." What you didn't realize in that moment was this—the devil just gave you homework. For the rest of the week, you'll be at home replaying that conversation in your head, totally convinced that the guy in question is your future spouse—and he knows it—or he at least suspects it. Why hasn't he asked you out or asked for your phone number? You reason within yourself that he's shy, he's afraid of rejection, or maybe he thinks you're dating another guy at the church (let's call him Mark) because Mark is always stopping you to talk about everything under the sun, including the puss-filled nodule on his upper back that the doctor had to drain and the ten dollar bill he found in his coat pocket after praying for a financial miracle. Howbeit, you are convinced that the other guy (we'll call him Chuck) is your man of God, and with every encounter you have with him, you get what feels all-the-more like confirmation. It gets so bad that you are now spending a great deal of your paycheck at boutiques, hair salons, nail shops, and at the mall altogether trying to look good for Chuck. Every Sunday, you go out of your way to impress Chuck, and on some Sundays, he compliments you or looks at you a few seconds longer than he ordinarily does. On other Sundays, you leave church feeling frustrated with Chuck because he didn't take a second look at you. In this, you have successfully gotten yourself entangled in a one-sided soul tie, and the binder that's holding you in that soul tie is delusion. Note: delusion has strengths; it starts off light and it serves as a warning to those who fall into the many traps of idolatry, but whenever the saints refuse to repent, God can and will turn them over to strong delusion.

One Sunday morning, you pull out your mirror to look at yourself before heading in the sanctuary. You are determined to get Chuck's attention this Sunday, because you are three Sundays away from Valentine's Day. That's when you hear Chuck's oh-so-familiar voice. He's loud, excited, obnoxious—he's being his usual self, except he's a little more animated. When you look up, you see Chuck slapping hands with Donald before hugging him. Behind Chuck stands a beautiful young lady wearing a striped black and white dress with pink accessories to compliment her bright pink lipstick. Who is she, and why is she standing behind Chuck like she knows him?! It's almost as if Heaven hears your thoughts because Chuck says to Donald, "Hey D, this is my fiance, Chantel.

Chantel, this is the man who stole the first girlfriend I ever had. This is Donald, but we call him D." Everyone laughs but you. "We were in the first grade, dude. Let it go," Donald laughs. "And I didn't steal your girlfriend. I flirted with her because she had candy in her backpack, and I wanted some; plus, she always had the big box of crayons. My parents only bought me the eight-count box."

Fiance. Fiance? Fiance?! You can't believe your ears, so you make your way over to join the conversation. "Chuck, did I just hear you say that you're engaged?" Chuck smiles uncomfortably, but he raises his shoulders, puts on a mask of confidence, and looks you square away in your eyes. "Yep, this is my wife-to-be, Chantel. Chantel, this is Brenda, one of my church sisters. She keeps me in line when you're not here, baby." After this brief introduction, Chuck's eyes dart across the room. "Hey, Joe!" he shouts, grabbing his girlfriend's hand and nearly dragging her away from you and towards one of the dullest and least entertaining men at the church—Mr. Joe. Nobody talks to Mr. Joe on purpose, after all, he's 72-years old, happily widowed, talkative, and he's always making inappropriate comments. It's obvious that

Chuck used Joe to evade that awkward moment with you, and he pays for it dearly. As you're walking away, you hear Mr. Joe saying the most off-the-wall thing to Chuck. He chuckles, "Oh, my boy, Chuck! Man, she's too skinny for you. You're gonna break that pretty little toothpick in half on y'all wedding night." He then shouts at Chantel, "Ma'am, don't you let this-here boy fornicate with you. Wait until y'all are married to do the do with him. In the meantime, go put some meat on your bones. If I were you, I'd be drinking protein drinks and pressing weights every day. I'd be off-roading and cross-country training ..."

Now, let's fast-forward to the end of service. You wave your final goodbyes to a few people as you enter your freshly washed car. You're sad, angry, distraught, and most of all, confused. How could Chuck be so cold? Why would he get your hopes up only to let you down? Is Chuck a false prophet? Wait, he's probably a narcissist. And does Chantel know that Chuck acts like a single man when she's not around? While in your vehicle, you begin to weep and pray, and midways through your prayer, you hear these words, "You're his wife. The other woman is a witch sent to destroy him. Pray for him. If he marries

27

her, he'll die. Chuck needs you in this hour." Amazed, your facial expression begins to change as you change lanes. "Wow, a witch?! Okay, it makes perfect sense now," you reason with yourself. So, you do what you were instructed to do. You begin to pray against Chuck's relationship and his upcoming marriage. Three Sundays later, you overhear Chuck asking your pastor for prayer. "The devil's attacking my relationship," he tells Pastor Andy. "Please keep us in prayer. Her dad is threatening to cut her off if she follows through with our wedding." You turn your head and smirk. "Thank you, Jesus," you murmur, believing that God is answering your prayers. He's not. The enemy is. Because those prayers are not righteous prayers. They are dark ones. What's happening is—Satan has lured you into the trap of witchcraft, and he now has you praying against a union that may have been established and ordained by God. This is a common story in today's dating climate. This happens when the spirit of delusion finds an idolatrous heart. This happens when believers don't bother to cast down imaginations that exalt themselves against God's knowledge; this happens when believers don't test the spirits by the Spirit. This happens when believers allow idolatrous thoughts to play in full-length, instead of praying against them. Now, this is not to say that everyone who's heard a voice claiming that another person is their spouse is the voice of a devil. This is to say that, in most cases, it is demonically orchestrated. Again, this is why the kingdom of darkness loves soul ties. You see, Satan and his imps know that getting you to tie your soul to someone else's soul is like tying a dog to a tree—you limit its movements, perspective, and you'll eventually break the dog's spirit. What you'd have left is a dog driven by its instinct to survive—to eat, sleep, protect its territory, and reproduce. You'd have a dog that would become more and more desperate and dangerous the longer it is chained to that tree. You'd also find a dog with a short life span. This is simply to demonstrate that the enemy uses soul ties to distract, harm, confuse, hinder, and break people. And he doesn't necessarily need us to get in relationships with other people if he can get us to operate in idolatry.

Nowadays, the spirit of delusion is commonplace, and if it continues to access and oppress God's people successfully, it won't be long before our society considers delusional people to be prophetic, discerning, and gifted souls, while rendering healthy, God-fearing, and sound-minded people who prefer prayer over prejudice, wisdom over whelms, sound logic over emotionalism, and patience over pressure to be weird, religious, and unreasonable. This is how the enemy works—when an issue arises in a generation or a society, the people who fight against that issue are viewed as enemies of progression. Over time, the issue gets more traction until it becomes commonplace, and then the world of psychology finds a term for the issue. After this, people who are bound by that issue (and the devils that came with it) start to normalize it, promoting the idea that anyone who promotes healing, deliverance, or Christian therapy is a religious, hate-filled, insensitive soul with prehistoric views. A generation or two later, the issue becomes normal, and the people who promote and follow God's Word are silenced. This is what the narrow path looks like. The broad path, on the other hand, forms when a crowd gathers around an issue, false love wages war with the God who is love, an idol is interwoven into the culture, and the people move further away from God, promoting the very thing that God hates. And to carry out this very sinister but well-thought-out plan, Satan needs soul ties. To bring about the spirit of delusion, Satan needs soul ties.

Oxford Languages defines the word "delusion" this way: "a false belief or judgment about external reality, held despite incontrovertible evidence to the contrary, occurring especially in mental conditions." The Greek word for "delusion" is "plané," and it means:

> "Cognate: 4106 plánē (a feminine noun derived from 4105 /planáō) – deviant behavior; a departure from what God says is true; an error (deception) which results in wandering (roaming into sin)."
> (Source: HELPS Word-studies)

Plainly put, delusion is deception, and it comes about when we give place to the enemy by not studying God's Word. After all, if you don't know the truth, you will easily believe a lie. So, when Satan goes about like a roaring lion looking for someone to devour, his menu typically consists of:

The biblically illiterate	Lukewarm believers
Idol worships	People bound by demonic

	contracts
People who rebel against God's Word	Prayerless souls
Prideful souls	People who live in victimhood
Hypocrites; friends of the world	Heathens

Don't get me wrong—he can, does, and will go after believers who love and fear the Lord, but he sends monitoring spirits after them so that he can know when and how to strike them. But Satan loves fast food as well; he's often looking for believers who are not satisfied with God alone. This is why God gave us a preventative medicine and the cure for idolatry, and that is Matthew 6:33, which reads, "But seek ye first the kingdom of God, and his righteousness; and all these things shall be added unto you." This is order. This is protocol. This is protection. This is how you guard your heart from ungodly soul ties. This is how you protect your mind from delusion that leads to strong delusion.

BINDING AGENTS

> The thief cometh not, but for to steal, and to kill, and to destroy: I am come that they might have life, and that they might have it more abundantly.
> John 10:10

An agent, according to Oxford Languages, is "a person who acts on behalf of another person or group." In this chapter, we are going to discuss the top three demonic agents that hell employs to establish, secure, and promote ungodly soul ties. These agents are, in no specific order:

The spirit of Leviathan
The spirit of Rejection
The spirit of Jezebel

These agents have specific roles in the lives of believers, and what works in our favor is the fact that they all have characteristics that make it easy for us to identify them. These characteristics have everything to do with their demonic assignments. Look at the tables below to see the characteristics of each devil to get a better understanding of how they operate.

Leviathan		
Pride	Ego	Vanity
Haughtiness	Offense	Selfishness

Rejection		
Fear	Insecurity	Self-Sabotage
People-Pleasing	Fear of Confrontation	Inability to Cleave

Jezebel		
Control	Manipulation	Intimidation
Witchcraft	Idolatry	Disorder

Of course, these are not the only agents that Satan uses to establish, strengthen, and break soul ties. These are the main ones. The rest include, but are not limited to:

Fear	Perversion	Offense
Mind Control	Obsession	Spirit Spouse

Unforgiveness	Python	Anger/Rage

I'll list a scenario, and I'll show you how each devil would use that scenario.

Nathan is frustrated with his wife because she won't stop checking his phone while he's asleep. Every time she's checked his phone, she's found another one of his dirty secrets. You see, Nathan is addicted to porn. He also frequents dating sites, reaches out to his exes, and frequents strip clubs. So, it goes without saying that Nathan is a nightmare to deal with, and his wife, Melissa, is at her wits' end.

One night, Melissa wakes up in the middle of the night, and she feels that ever-so-overwhelming urge to check her husband's phone, so she gives in. She types in his passcode, and once the screen clears, Melissa heads straight over to Nathan's text messages. There, she finds a text thread between Nathan and his ex, Briana. The text messages were sexually charged, with Nathan sending his ex a lot of shirtless pictures of himself lying on his bed. One message even read, "When I'm with her, I pretend that I'm with you. Is that weird?" Angry and upset, Melissa rushes back to the bedroom, snatches the covers off of Nathan as she begins to scream at the top of her lungs. Nathan begins to have a demonic episode. Let's review how Leviathan, Rejection and Jezebel would respond, depending on which devil is surfacing at that time.

Leviathan

- "I told you to stop checking my phone! That's what you get for being nosy!"
- "Apologize for what?! I didn't do anything wrong!"
- "Oh well. What's next?"
- "I want a divorce!"

Rejection

- "You were just looking for a reason to leave me. You didn't have to take it to that length. I wish you would have just left."
- "I only reached out to her because you make me feel invisible."
- "Go ahead and read me the benediction!"
- "I knew it. You're going to leave me like everyone else does."

Jezebel

- "You can leave, but the kids are going to stay here with me!"
- "You're not going anywhere!"
- "I'll call your job and tell them how you sometimes come home without clocking out!"
- "Please don't leave me. I'll kill myself if you leave me."

Each type of spirit has patterns of behavior that are easily recognizable once you familiarize yourself with it. So, in the next few chapters, we will discuss these binding agents in greater detail.

The Spirit of Leviathan

> Thou brakest the heads of leviathan in pieces, and gavest
> him to be meat to the people inhabiting the wilderness.
> Psalm 74:14

Understand that we aren't as tied to people as we are to
principles. The ties that hold us in place are typically
principles and plans. Think of it this way—Billy Bob and
Megan believe that space aliens exist; they also believe
that the government is working with those aliens, they
control the weather, and that many of their favorite
celebrities who have reportedly passed on are
somewhere on a foreign and private island living under a
different name. According to Oxford Languages, the
word "principle" means, "a fundamental truth or
proposition that serves as the foundation for a system
of belief or behavior or for a chain of reasoning." This is
to say that Billy and Megan's beliefs have set the stage
for a group of principles that they've chosen to live and
abide by. Consequently, what will tie these two lovers
together is a group of theories, and these theories will

set the stage for their future plans. If the couple were to break up without changing their minds, they would be broken up physically, but mentally, morally, and physically, they will still be "one." This has everything to do with the fact that some of their principal beliefs are still in alignment. So, when Megan goes to an alien convention, she will think of Billy. When Billy finds himself wanting to talk about what the news has reported as a flying object hoovering over Pakistan, he'll likely think of Megan. He may even text or call her because the two of them have something in common. Of course, this will bring about the question— what if me and my ex don't believe in anything as outlandish as the aforementioned example? What if we are two believers who love the Lord, but simply could not get along? The answer is simple. If the both of you truly agreed with God, you'd still be together because you would unite in Him. However, there was a core principle that one of you had that the other party did not share. And whatever this belief was—it was far more important to you or your former partner than the marriage itself. It was a deal-breaker, and nine times out of ten, one or both of you were wrestling with the Leviathan spirit. Here are a few facts about the Leviathan spirit:

1. He is a covenant-breaking spirit.
2. He is a twisting spirit (see Isaiah 27:1).
3. He is the king of the proud (see Job 41:34).
4. His scales are so closely knit together that it is hard to penetrate him (see Job 41:15-17).

The spirit of Leviathan is behind:

1. Divorce.
2. Church hopping.
3. Church splitting.
4. Failed friendships.
5. Damaged families.
6. Failed attempts to connect.
7. Broken relationships.

This wicked spirit damages and destroys relationships by encouraging its hosts to operate in pride; this is because Leviathan understands that:

- Pride goeth before destruction, and an haughty spirit before a fall (see Proverbs 16:18).
- God resisteth the proud, but giveth grace unto the humble (see James 4:6).

Satan and his army are defeated foes, so he understands that it would be nearly impossible for them, outside of a legality, to kill, steal, and destroy God's people. Therefore, he still pulls the same wild card that he pulled on Eve. He tempts the people of God to step outside of God's will, where he has dominion. And since it is illegal for us to operate outside of God's will, Satan then uses that crime to accuse and arrest us. All the same, according to the scriptures, Leviathan (one of Satan's favorite henchmen) is a twisting spirit. In this, he is likened to an alligator or a crocodile. Consider how these reptiles kill their prey. They will either:

1. Drag their prey into the water and drown them. When this happens, the prey has to be near the water. This typically happens when an animal nears a body of water to take a drink.

2. Grab one of the limbs of the animal it wants to consume, and then start a death-roll, thus severing the animal's limb from its body. This causes the animal to bleed to death or go into cardiac arrest.

Alligators and crocodiles are opportunistic feeders,

meaning they'll eat any animal that presents itself; they won't go out looking for prey. Instead, they'll readily eat whatever avails itself to them, whether that animal is a bird, frog, snake, deer, antelope, turtle, etc. For large animals, the alligator loves to drag them outside of their domain and into the water, where the reptilian creature has the upper hand. This is similar to what Satan does. He loves to get God's people outside of God's will or, at minimum, playing around at the border between sin and righteousness (lukewarm), where he lies in wait ready to strike when the opportunity presents itself. When the prey isn't too close to the water, alligators and crocodiles prefer the death-roll; in this, they twist one of the limbs off their prey. This is what the Leviathan spirit does. It twists the truth; this is how it breaks covenants. For example, imagine arguing with a spouse of yours because you found out that your spouse has been chatting online with his or her ex. You confront your significant other, and instead of repenting, coming clean, and seeking wise counsel, your spouse decides to argue with you. You hear:

- "Why were you checking my inbox in the first place?!"

- "What were you looking for on my computer?!"
- "My Mom always said that if you go looking for trouble, you will surely find it! You went looking for it, so here we are!"
- "Let me look at your inbox messages! I'm sure you haven't been an angel!"

After this, the gaslighting may start. Your spouse may then say:

- "Your trust issues are what's destroying this marriage!"
- "Didn't your Mom say that you used to take medicine for anxiety? Are you okay, right now? Did that demon come back?"
- "Be truthful with me. Have you ever been diagnosed with anything other than anxiety?"
- "I didn't reach out to my ex! The message you saw was an old one! You just saw it today because I was checking my message requests on Facebook!"
- "You're just like my ex! Remember, I told you that my ex destroyed our relationship with his insecurities!"

And finally, your spouse may feel like he or she has a good enough lie to tell you.

"Okay, I'll tell you the truth. I did reach out to Brenda today, but only because I saw that she had messaged me. We started chatting, and she was updating me regarding matters that took place in her family, and I didn't think anything was wrong with having a one-time chat with her. It was purely innocent! What's worse is, I was literally feeling sad, depressed, and a little suicidal today, but she cheered me up. That's how I know that it was God who had her to inbox me, after all, you were probably off somewhere looking out for yourself. I just needed someone to talk to, and I didn't want to burden you with my issues since you told me last month that I whined about everything, and just yesterday, you seemed to be annoyed when I sat next to you." From here, he or she may start to play the victim, saying things like, "People always misunderstand me" or "I feel like no one ever listens to me." After this, your spouse may begin to cry in an attempt to shift your attention away from their ex and place it on themselves.

These are all manifestations of pride, wherein, you'll

find:

Pride	Self-pity
Ego	Self-worship (sin)
Vanity	Offense
Self-exaltation	Unforgiveness
Entitlement	Selfish ambition
Individualism	Haughtiness
Self-preservation	Self-reliance

What do you notice about most of the items on the above list? They start with "self." As a matter of fact, sin in plain terms is nothing but self-worship. It is a form of idolatry. Idolatry is not just the worship of something external; it starts with the worship of self, whereas, you'll worship or exalt your plans and preferences over God's will, exalt your feelings over how God feels, and exalt your fears and faults over God's Word. This creates a need, a hunger, and a void in the soul. Once Satan creates this emptiness, he will then play commercials in your mind of what you'll need to do to satisfy the hunger within. These commercials will promote sin, selfish-ambition, haughtiness, evil associations, etc. This is why 2 Corinthians 10:5 states, "Casting down imaginations, and every high thing that exalteth itself against the knowledge of God, and bringing into captivity every thought to the obedience of Christ." Read this carefully—whatever you don't cast down will ultimately have to be cast out.

Going back to the example of the prideful spouse, what the enemy would do to destroy your marriage (if he could) would be to set the stage for individualism. You see, the two of you are supposed to operate as a unit; you're supposed to move in unity. Howbeit, if one person starts defending himself or herself, being self-centered or vain, what would then happen would be the other spouse would feel exposed, uncovered, and devalued. Consequently, that spouse would start to look out for himself or herself, so instead of operating as a unit, the both of you would begin to operate individually. Within the word "individual" is the prefix of divide, divination, and divorce which, of course, is "div." Mark 3:25 warns, "And if a house be divided against itself, that house cannot stand." In other words, the household would fall apart at the seams. This is where Leviathan draws its strength; it gets its best grip in the void. What this means is, it is difficult and oftentimes impossible for Leviathan to attack a unified couple, especially if that couple is united in Christ. However, if a house is divided, Leviathan will have dominion over that household.

- **Matthew 18:19-20:** Again I say unto you, that if two of you shall agree on earth as touching any thing that they shall ask, it shall be done for them of my Father which is in heaven. For where two or three are gathered together in my name, there am I in the midst of them.

- **Ecclesiastes 4:9-12:** Two are better than one; because they have a good reward for their labor. For if they fall, the one will lift up his fellow: but woe to him that is alone when he falleth; for he hath not another to help him up. Again, if two lie together, then they have heat: but how can one be warm alone? And if one prevail against him, two shall withstand him; and a threefold cord is not quickly broken.

Leviathan has to split a home in order to destroy it, and to do this, he always goes after the head of the home.

The head of any given household or structure is known as the strongman. Yes, this is even true when it comes to demonic networks; there is always a strongman at play. Mark 3:27 reads, "No man can enter into a strong man's house, and spoil his goods, except he will first bind the strong man; and then he will spoil his house." What Leviathan (and other unclean spirits) seek to do is to become the strongman by binding the strongman, and then taking his place. He doesn't have to necessarily remove the strongman, he simply needs to bring him under his authority; this is why he is known as the "king of the children of pride."

Again, what does any of this have to do with soul ties? Demons love ungodly soul ties, and Leviathan loves to break Godly soul ties so that he can establish ungodly ones. He also loves to use ungodly soul ties to create the infamous "type" that we hear so much about. Most people claim to have a type, not realizing that (in most cases), our types are nothing but people who host spirits that we are familiar with. This is why we feel comfortable around them; they don't necessarily feel like strangers to us. Instead, they feel "safe." Whenever we have a type, we are most likely to:

1. Move fast in the relationship.
2. Engage in illegal sexual activity with the person.
3. Give that person access to the intimate and sacred spaces in our lives.
4. Give that person access to our children prematurely.
5. Give that person access to our resources.
6. Not test the spirit behind that individual.
7. Run past the speed limit of true love and straight into the arms of lust, obsession, and idolatry.

And here's how Leviathan plays the game. He encourages the people under his authority to rush into relationships, give a sin offering (this allows him to lord himself over the relationship), and give that person a seat in our hearts that was supposed to be reserved for God. From there, God's hand lifts off of the relationship, Leviathan takes his place in the relationship, and he then uses the relationship to bruise, break, and bring both parties under his control all the more. This is because he breaks the relationship, but not necessarily the soul tie. You see, the objective is to have both parties going from one relationship to another with an inability to cleave. This way, all of their relationships will fail, but the soul ties formed in these relationships will allow him to have access to more and more people. This is how he builds his kingdom! All the same, he can build a system called unforgiveness, whereas one of both of the parties involved in the relationship in question will have Satan's heart towards their former lovers. That's all unforgiveness is after all! God wants us to have His heart towards His people and the people in the world, but unforgiveness sets the stage for anyone bound by it to have Satan's heart, wishes, plans, and desires for the person who hurt, rejected, persecuted, abandoned, and humiliated them. It's nearly the perfect plan! One sin sets the stage for another sin, and before long, Leviathan will have an empire filled with hurt, bitter, and rejected people who refuse to take accountability for their own roles in their pain. Instead, they overly focus on their intentions and how well they treated the people who'd hurt them, totally disregarding the fact that they repeatedly sinned against God for these people. This keeps them in a state of mind called victimhood, wherein they come to believe that they have been wronged or mismanaged, thus disregarding the principles of sowing and reaping. If you sin against God to get in a relationship, you will reap what the world refers to as consequences. Notice that the word "sequence" is in consequence. Oxford Languages defines the word "sequence" this way:

1. a particular order in which related events, movements, or things follow each other.
2. a set of related events, movements, or things that follow each other in a particular order.

Understand that the spirit realm is like a mirror. What you do on one side of it will reflect itself on the other side. So, what you do to God, someone will ultimately do to you. If you're not faithful to God, you will reap a partner who is unfaithful to you. If you idolize your plans over God's plans, you will likely reap a partner who's selfish ⋯ someone who believes that his plans or her plans are superior to your own. And when Leviathan has dominion over a relationship, he will use that relationship to lead the parties in it further and further away from Christ. If one of the people involved in that relationship refuses to comply with his demands, he'll use the other partner to shift the atmosphere in their home from peaceful to demonic. In other words, he'll rob his offender of their peace. This is why the enemy loves soul ties; they are like chains tied to the back of a pickup truck, designed to help pull or drag his people out of the relationships that they're in when those relationships no longer serve him or when he decides that he needs one or both parties to pair up with other people. Keep this in mind—to a demon, you are nothing but an object. You are a means to an end.

THE SPIRIT OF REJECTION

> If the world hate you, ye know that it hated me before it
> hated you.
> John 15:18

The spirit of rejection is so common in the United States
and abroad that most of the people we come in contact
with on a daily basis are wrestling with it. Some more
than others, of course. I have witnessed firsthand that
some people are so bound by the system and spirit of
rejection that they see promotion as rejection. All the
same, some people think that you are supposed to
tolerate their bad behavior, rude attitudes, poor
choices, and narcissistic ways if they've gone out of
their way to be nice to you or help you with something.
There's no getting around this. You can either host them
for the rest of their lives and walk on eggshells with
them, being extremely careful that you don't fracture
their egos or you can do what's best for them—kick
them out of your life and wish them the best. If you do
the latter,they will toss you into the same category that

they've tossed their parents, exes, and pastors into, and that category is that of an enemy. They will see you as another person who came into their lives, took advantage of them, and then just threw them away like trash. And while this may be something they've experienced with others, every failed (or successful) relationship that they've had didn't necessarily end prematurely. The problem is their perception of rejection, their unrealistic expectations, and the mother/father wounds that they have. Believe it or not, these open wounds are oftentimes behind these three facts:

1. They wear their hearts on their sleeves.
2. They love hard.
3. They are incredibly loyal to people.

This sounds great; right?! Wouldn't you want someone in your life who embodied those three traits? Most people think they do; that is until they start realizing that:

1. Those wounds were created by voids and/or trauma.
2. Every void is God-sized.
3. When you play God in someone's life, they will

eventually revere you as the devil because you won't be able to heal, satisfy, or fill their voids.

4. The force behind their loyalty is an actual spirit; it is a demon called Rejection.
5. You can't talk a demon out of being a demon. In other words, the rejected soul will continue to harass, punish, and mistreat their lovers until they die, divorce, or adjust to the treatment.

Spirits like to serve as deities, and every deity requires offerings. And get this—a deity can accept or reject an offering, and every spirit is the embodiment of its name. For example, the spirit of anger is an angry spirit, and whenever it surfaces, it provokes its host to anger; this is how it expresses itself. Rejection is no different. This particular spirit is the very picture of the adage "hurt people hurt people." This is to say that the spirit of rejection feels the weight of God's rejection; it is a whiny, dejected spirit, and whenever it takes a front-row seat in its hosts' lives, it causes them to feel what it feels—rejected, overlooked, misunderstood, unwanted, unappreciated, taken advantage of, unfairly judged, etc. So, when a host is having an episode of rejection, what's happening in that moment is that the spirit of rejection needs to be fed. And just like you feed the devil of anger by allowing it to scream, throw things around, threaten people, or maybe even get violent, the spirit of rejection expresses itself by causing its host to reject others (temporarily or permanently), sabotage their relationships by being too clingy, needy, and insecure; then again, it likes to bring the other party under its control by holding the rejected soul over their heads and forcing them to submit to the other party's demands. This may look like, for example, a rejected wife threatening to divorce her husband because he refuses to cut ties with his family, move to another state, allow her to stay out late unquestioned, or do whatsoever she demands. She may not outright say, "If you don't stop asking me where I've been, I'm going to file for divorce." Instead, she may make a few statements and leave them up to the husband for interpretation. For example, she may say, "I don't think I can continue living like this. I'm a grown woman. I already have two parents; I don't need you to be a third. I think we may need some time apart." If these words don't put fear in her husband, she may then respond by packing her bags and leaving him—temporarily. The objective is to scare him into submission.

But why are we talking about the spirit of rejection? Because it's the culprit behind the many soul ties that we are going to be discussing. I want you to see a soul tie as a chain, and while it doesn't look like a chain, a rope, or an umbilical cord, it does act as such. It pulls on the hearts and souls of people; it chains people to perspectives, relationships, and fears, and worst of it, it sets the stage for the worst type of soul tie that anyone can have, and that is a soul tie called Idolatry.

But wait! How does someone end up bound by the spirit of rejection? This foul spirit typically enters through:
1. Parental rejection.
2. Peer rejection.
3. The rejection of a romantic partner; this includes divorce.
4. Societal rejection (this includes racism, classism, and every line that divides the human race).
5. Cultural rejection.
6. Media (trends, beauty standards, and norms

established by music, movies, social media, and every medium that serves as a communicator between two worlds or realms).

All the same, there are different types of rejection. They include:

1. **Actual rejection:** This happens when a person is truly rejected by other people. In other words, the people in question are placing a boundary, a standard, or a closed door in front of the individual. Please note that the person rejecting the other soul isn't always a villain. In many cases, they are protecting themselves from what they see, believe, or perceive.

2. **Perceived rejection:** In this, the rejected soul feels like he or she is being pushed away, denied access, or judged because the individual in question is not getting the response that he or she wants to receive. However, the other party may be inviting the individual into a role that the rejected soul does not want to have. A great example of this is when someone wants to be your best friend, and that person goes out of his or her

way to get close to you far too fast, and you put up a speed limit that disables their progress. In this, you invite them into your life to be nothing more than a sister in Christ—for now. You simply want to get to know them better, but the rejected party is hellbent on being your bestie. Consequently, he or she may walk away feeling judged, mishandled, and rejected ⋯ not because you've wronged them, but because they interpreted your boundary as you having some type of prejudice or preconceived notion about them. The rejected party may then start to question why you're not allowing them to get the access that they want, and the spirit of rejection will utilize that moment to lie to them and sow more discord. So, let's say that a woman named Yolanda had gone out of her way to get close to you, but you keep rejecting her invitations to lunch, you keep your phone calls relatively short, you don't open up to her about your personal life, and you don't answer a lot of her calls. However, you are friendly and welcoming towards her, but she wants more. Let's say that the two of you met at church. Chances are, she will pay close attention to the people you're close to or incredibly friendly towards at the church, and she will likely come to the conclusion that one of the women or men who's not too fond of her has spoken reproachfully about her to you. Offended, she may take to Facebook with a post that reads like, "People these days don't use the good sense that the Lord gave them! If you believe what other folks say about people that you don't know, you just might miss out on a blessing!" If that post doesn't get the response she wants, she may come back and share someone else's status that reads, for example, "Don't listen to what a jealous person says about another person! Get to know people for yourself, and then develop your own opinion of them! If you keep listening to jealous people, it's only a matter of time before they'll take you down with them!" If you were to follow the link to the original post, you would find the rejected soul in the comment section saying, "Preach!" or "Whew!" They may even follow up with a few emojis designed to show their agreement. Then again, they may follow up in the comment section with, "Confirmation!" or "Man of God, I am literally experiencing this right now! Thank you for letting the Lord use you!"

3. **Justified rejection:** Let's face it. We can't all have what we want, when we want it, or how we want it. And truth be told, some of the most toxic, unhealed, controlling, manipulative, and destructive people will go out of their way to get access to anyone they believe will be of benefit to them. This is because many of these souls are narcissistic, either covertly or overtly. And entitlement does not equal access. So, we oftentimes reject people because they are dangerous to be around. Just like we all know the symptoms of the common cold, a stomach virus, or the symptoms of the flu, we should also know the symptoms of toxic behaviors. I've given people access to me, and then after dealing with them, I've withdrawn that access because of their toxic ways. This is to say that just because someone has managed to gain access to your life doesn't mean that you have to keep them in your life. What

you'll come to learn (if you haven't learned this already) is that some people are very cunning; they hide behind flattery, nice gestures, bubbly personalities, and their God-given gifts. And let's be honest—we don't always test the spirits in people before we give them access to our lives. Consequently, over time, we've all had to reject people who've successfully integrated into our lives, just as we've had to reject people who've gone out of their way to get access to her, and we were justified in doing so. All the same, we've been justifiably rejected by others as well.

4. **Biased rejection:** Humans are creatures of familiarity. We tend to want to be around people who remind us of the folks that we've been around. We look for certain traits, characteristics, and mannerisms in the people we invite into our lives—for the most part. Then again, we tend to avoid people who have certain traits, characteristics, mannerisms, belief systems, and whatever it is that we deem to be "normal" or desirable. This is to say that we often reject people because of our biases, and we are rejected

by people who are biased. For example, I think that most Americans can attest to this fact—there are girls (women even) who only hang around other girls who fit a certain aesthetic. As silly and narcissistic as this may be, we've all met women who only befriend women who are, by societal norms, considered to be beautiful. Consider colorism. In the African American community, there are fair-skinned women who will only befriend fair-skinned women. In the Caucasian community, there are women who will only befriend women who are a size two or a size four, at most, and the women they befriend have to be relatively or incredibly vain. This sets the stage for biased rejection, whereas, a woman who is a size eight might try to befriend a group of girls, and find herself not only being rejected, but bullied. Then again, if she's attractive enough, rich enough, or connected to powerful people, the ladies may invite her into their circle, where they will start their campaign to help her lose the excess weight.

We're talking about these forms of rejection because every soul tie, once strained or broken, sets the stage for the spirit of rejection to enter into our lives or the lives of others. Every attraction or pull that we experience towards others can, does, and will set the stage for a soul tie.

Ultimately, rejection traces its way back to Eden, but the spirit of rejection can be traced back to the moment when Satan deceived a third of God's angels. In this, the angels that sided with Satan simultaneously rejected the Most High God, and this caused them to be rejected by God. Therefore, every demon that exists feels and is rejected by God, but the spirit of rejection embodies that rejection. Just like Jesus bore our sins for us, the spirit of rejection carries the weight of God's rejection, and it goes out of its way to relieve itself by making God's people feel rejected by God and rejected by the people they love, the people they want to love, and the people who once loved them. Please understand that the weight of rejection is unbearable; this is why it has to be expressed and shared, so whenever you feel rejected, you will find a way to relieve yourself of the disappointment, the hurt, the shame, the guilt, and every emotion associated with rejection. You may try to share those emotions with others by communicating to them, or you may hurt, reject, or use someone's issue of rejection against them in an attempt to get them to understand how you feel. Either way, this is demonic and ungodly, and it should be addressed through Bible study, therapy, and deliverance.

THE SPIRIT OF JEZEBEL

> And it came to pass, when Joram saw Jehu, that he said, Is it peace, Jehu? And he answered, What peace, so long as the whoredoms of thy mother Jezebel and her witchcrafts are so many?
>
> 2 Kings 9:22

If you know the story of Jezebel, as well as God's judgment for the spirit of Jezebel and those who tolerate her, you'd know the following about Jezebel:

1. She is a pagan worshiper.
2. She is polytheistic.
3. She hates the prophets of God.
4. She is seductive.
5. She is a witch.
6. She has infiltrated the 5-fold.
7. She is a ruler.
8. She is manipulative.
9. She is a murderer.

There's a lot more to say about this wicked woman, but

we all know her fate; she was tossed out of the window of her castle by her eunuchs, the dogs came and ate her flesh, and Jehu had her servants to bury what was left of her. But what you might not know is this—the spirit that was in her was an ancient devil. As a matter of fact, that spirit once inhabited Cain; it was also hosted by Delilah, Haman, Abimilech, King Herod, Herodias, Athaliah, Absalom, Pharaoh, King Saul, and the list goes on. Understand this—demons are fallen angels who lost their original names in Heaven; for example, Lucifer is now known as Satan. The word "Satan" isn't necessarily a name, it means "adversary," so God literally refers to Satan as His enemy. Imagine hearing God repeatedly say to a person, "Hey, enemy of mine. What are you up to today?" All the same, each fallen angel, when it was in Heaven, had a function. For example, there were angels that served as watchers, warriors, messengers, etc., and the way they were designed was in direct correlation to their purpose. So, when they fell, they didn't necessarily lose their design, they lost:

1. God's trust.
2. Their roles and positions.
3. Eternity with God.

4. God's presence.

5. The benefits of God's presence.

Think of it this way. God is Abba. The word "Abba" means "Father." It also means "Source." We know that God is the source of all power; this is why He is all-powerful. So, imagine that He is this huge power source; as a matter of fact, He is the only power source. Now, imagine that demons are like cell phones. They have to plug into Him to be empowered, and once they are unplugged, they can function, perform, and do what they were designed to do, but whenever they start to power down, they have to go back to the Source and plug themselves in again. Envision God ripping all of their cords out and casting them out of His presence. Get this—they still had a measure of power left; the ones that didn't were cast into outer darkness. We were made in the image of God, but because of our sins, we were cast away from God too, but God gave us a Savior, so we are able to plug into Him through His Son, Christ Jesus. Imagine demons walking around the Earth and they see these creatures filled with the light of God, some more than others. You have the unbeliever who has enough light to find God, and you have the believer who has enough light to lead others to God. What's all the more amazing is the fact that we are all plugged into God, so while He is the Source, we serve as resources or recycled power. A weary demon that's been powering down, not able to plug into the Source sees you and me as plug-and-play stations. This is why they seek to plug themselves into us, but in order for this to happen, we have to come into agreement with them; we have to go into sin. That's where the 6,000-60,000 negative thoughts a day that the world of psychology say that we all have come into play. To demons, we are real estate; we are buildings filled with rooms, levels, and possibilities. So, let's say that a demon successfully entered a man. That demon has to be fed; it has to be empowered, so to get its food, it has to get that man to surrender his authority through sin, fear, doubt, rebellion, procrastination, doubt, etc. And that devil doesn't want to have to tempt that man every single day. No, demons love to create structures and systems called strongholds. A stronghold, according to Oxford Languages, is "a place where a particular cause or belief is strongly defended or upheld." In other words, demons have to infiltrate your belief system by introducing you to lies. Each lie sets the stage for another lie; it invites in some of the lies that come into the waiting room of your mind every day, all the while repelling and rejecting the truth.

Jezebel's job is to lead God's people astray using seduction, manipulation, intimidation, domination, witchcraft, mind control, and fear. As a matter of fact, Jezebel is skilled at forming soul ties with people. Someone bound by this spirit will:

1. Run past the speed limit of love in an attempt to form an in-depth, close-knit, and intimate relationship with you.
2. Flatter you to get access to your heart, your trust, and whatever else it is that they are eyeing in your life.
3. Show up for you where others have failed you.

But make no mistake about it—someone bound by the Jezebel spirit has little to no ability to love anyone outside of themselves, and even the love they give themselves is not true love. It's self-obsession. They generalize and objectify people. In other words, to them, you are but a means to an end. These individuals are either narcissists or they are incredibly narcissistic. They treat soul ties like lassos. Anytime they come in contact with people who they believe will be of some benefit to them, they will try to soul tie themselves to those people, and again, when they want to form a soul tie with you, they will often try to find the areas of your soul that are either weak or rich. When they focus on the weak areas, they will, without your permission, try to exalt themselves as an adviser, wise counselor, or leader in your life. When they focus on your rich areas, they will disguise themselves as little sisters or brothers in the Lord, mentees, or lost sheep. This is false humility, and this particular tactic is often used by the covert narcissist and covertly narcissistic individuals. They'll use this tactic to get access to your heart, but as the soul tie forms and gets stronger, you'll notice that they'll start to focus on areas in your life that are underdeveloped, dark, fractured, or filled with wrong information, and they'll start advising you in those areas. It'll start off subtle. Let's say that the area that you need to develop in is with your eating habits, but they are no health coach. They've just spent more

time in the gym and they have a little more discipline
than you in the area of nutrition. If their initial interest
was getting you to help them get closer to God, you'll
notice that they don't talk too much about building their
relationship with Him anymore. As a matter of fact, they
will seem almost offended when you try to coach them in
that area. Instead, they may call you and lead with, "Did
you go to the gym today? Remember what I told you! You
are too invaluable to the body of Christ to eat yourself
into an early grave!" This sounds great; it sounds like
love, but this is all centered around control. Note: if the
person is passionate about health or they happen to be a
health coach, personal trainer, or gym-head (someone
who is addicted to the gym, not just a seasonal gym
attendant), it is normal for them to start focusing on
helping you to get to a better place physically. However,
if they are no longer interested in getting closer to God,
please know that you're likely dealing with a bound
person who is trying to lead you, and whenever a bound
person leads another person, they will lead that person
astray. Matthew 15:14 reads, "Let them alone: they be
blind leaders of the blind. And if the blind lead the blind,
both shall fall into the ditch."

Unfortunately, as a leader, I've had my fair share of encounters with people who were bound by this spirit, and most of them were confirmed cases, meaning either I'd taken them through deliverance from Jezebel before or they went elsewhere and received deliverance from the spirit of Jezebel. The issue was that they kept allowing that spirit to reenter them. What I soon discovered was that people who wrestle with that spirit need way more than deliverance. They need extensive therapy, and they also have to learn how to live without that devil. They have to:

- Release their Ahabs. In other words, whomever it is that they've mastered controlling, they have to release their hold and control on that person, and that's no easy task for someone who's bound by Jezebel.
- Overcome their desire to be in control or to have their way.
- Overcome the spirit and the system of rejection.
- Heal so the word "no" doesn't feel like they're being judged, abused, mismanaged, mishandled, persecuted, or rejected.
- Come out of victimhood.

- Forgive the people who've hurt, abused, rejected, or abandoned them.
- Learn to take accountability for their actions.
- Study the Word so they can grow up in the areas where they are underdeveloped and immature.
- Seek the Lord daily and put Him first.
- Learn to cast down imaginations and every high thing that exalts itself against the knowledge of God, and bring into captivity every thought to the obedience of Christ.
- Trust the Lord and lean not to their own understanding.
- Come out of idolatry.
- Use their giftings, their talents, and their intelligence for good, and not to manipulate and control people.
- Put and keep God first.

There is a spectrum of narcissism, and get this—every human being is on this spectrum. This is because of our sin nature. On the far left of this spectrum are narcissists; on the far right of this spectrum are mere humans with normalized narcissism. When we're born, we're at the center of this spectrum because children are naturally narcissistic. No, this doesn't mean that they are evil or that they are bound by the Jezebel spirit. This simply means that they are self-centered, self-absorbed, and selfish; they have to be. But as they age, parents should notice them becoming less and less self-centered. I think about what I call the potato chip test. It's when you hand a toddler a huge bag of potato chips, and then you ask for a chip. When the child shares a chip with you without crying if you take or bite it, that's a sign that the child is maturing. No, they won't be fully mature anytime soon, but they are developing, and that's great! I think a better example would be a trend that recently went viral on social media. Parents would sit their children at a counter or a table, and film their toddlers' responses to one of the parents (mostly the mother) not having a cookie on her plate. The way this went was—the father would sit on one side of the child, the mother would sit on the other side of the child, and of course, the child would be seated in the center. In front of each person would be a plate with another plate or napkin on top. The test would start off with the father pulling the napkin off his plate, revealing that he had a cookie on his plate. The trio would celebrate, and then the parents would happily say to the child, "Your turn." The child would then pull the napkin off of his or her plate, revealing that they had two cookies, to the child's surprise. The noticeably elated child would then celebrate before they all turned their attention to the final party—the child's mother. She would then take the napkin off her plate, revealing that she didn't have any cookies at all. This was a test to see how each child responded. Some children would show a measure of empathy towards their mothers, but they wouldn't offer her one of the two cookies on their plates. Some children wouldn't show any empathy at all; instead, they found it humorous that their mothers didn't have any cookies. Lastly, there were children who were incredibly empathetic. One child even cried before grabbing a cookie off his plate and placing it on his mother's plate. The children who shared their cookies with their mothers (or fathers) showed signs that they were maturing or developing at a healthy rate. Howbeit, we can't judge the ones who didn't show signs of empathy because children don't all mature at the same rate. However, over time, if they still don't show signs of empathy, the parents would need to evaluate their parenting and they may have to have their children evaluated. They may have to evaluate their children's surroundings, what others are teaching and allowing the children to think, believe, and do, and they may have to evaluate what their children are consuming media-wise. Either way, an evaluation should be done if their children are still showing signs of incredible selfishness when most children are socializing well with other children. This is to say that children start in the middle of the spectrum, but should move towards the right of the spectrum as they grow older. This is why you'll notice that people compare narcissists to children; they tend to have tantrums and emotional outbursts, and they have heightened responses to them not getting their way.

Jezebel loves to connect herself to God's prophets and prophetic people. Yes, this spirit can be in a man, so don't let the gender-language confuse you. When you have a call on your life, especially when you're incredibly prophetic or you are called to the office of the prophet, you will attract narcissists and incredibly narcissistic people. That's because Jezebel's assignment is to destroy God's prophets, and she does this from the inside out. Jezebel seeks people who fall in love easily, people who place their desires, feelings, and plans over God's will. In other words, the spirit of Jezebel looks for idol worshipers and people who are prone to idolatry, after all, the narcissist is your reward for idolatry. Demons think in legalities and generations. They think in legalities, meaning, they are always looking for a legal right to bind a person or they will go out of their way to get people to bind themselves legally to them. To do this, they need to get the people in question to sin against God, especially with the people they want to use to bind them. This is the sin offering, and with this offering, the enemy is able to establish ungodly agreements between souls. These ungodly soul ties bind one person to another person who's bound to other people who're bound to other people; this chain stretches from one city to the next, one state to another, and one generation to another. It's a continuum that allows the demonic world to travel at will between souls. The overall job of Jezebel is to gain souls for Ahab's harem. These unwitting Baal worshipers would become meat for the enemy.

- **Psalm 14:4:** Have all the workers of iniquity no knowledge? Who eat up my people as they eat bread, and call not upon the LORD.
- **1 Peter 5:8:** Be sober, be vigilant; because your adversary the devil, as a roaring lion, walketh about, seeking whom he may devour.

Satan goes about seeking whom he MAY devour, which means that he can't devour everyone. He looks for people with uncrucified flesh; he looks for people who have the appearance of godliness but deny the power thereof. He looks for people with little faith and big idols. He looks for people with voids, unforgiveness, wounded hearts, and ungodly ambition. And when he finds these types of people, he uses monitoring spirits to study them; this way, he'll know which demon to send their way, whether that demonized person is bound by Jezebel, Ahab, fear, pride, lust, etc. What you struggle with will determine what Satan throws at you.

The problem isn't the fact that Jezebel is attracted to you (if that spirit tends to come after you). The real problem is you being attracted to people who have this spirit. This means there is a side of you that is void of God; there is a side of you that is unhealed. Then again, there is a side of you that is filled with idolatry. This means that you possess something that belongs to the kingdom of darkness, and Jezebel has a legal right to come after whatever it is that you are in possession of, after all, two can only walk together if they are in agreement (see Amos 3:3). Yes, you will likely get your fair share of broken souls looking to connect with you, and they will attempt to seduce you, flatter you, love-bomb you or scare you into forming a relationship with them. And if you give them access to your mind, your heart, or your plans, they will look for errors in your life, and get this, you're human, so there are some areas of your life that need healing and developing. If and when they find those areas, they will try to help you in those areas. The goal is to get you to:

1. See how beneficial it is for you to have whatever it is that you've been lacking.
2. Form a dependency or build a lifestyle around your newfound strength.
3. Grow your confidence based on whatever it is that

they've added to your life.

4. Use all of the above as a mechanism of control by threatening to walk away or deprive you of said benefit whenever you don't comply with their "suggestions" or demands.

5. Convince you that they have your best interest in mind; this way, they can disguise their abuse as love.

Marriage and Divorce

> The wife is bound by the law as long as her husband liveth; but if her husband be dead, she is at liberty to be married to whom she will; only in the Lord.
>
> 1 Corinthians 7:39

Get this—a soul tie formed with a narcissist will eventually harden and become a yoke. What's the difference between a soul tie and a yoke? A soul tie is something that ties two souls together, but a yoke is a legally binding tie or contract that connects two souls together. You can sever a soul tie by repenting, but you'll typically have to fast and pray to break a yoke since yokes are contractual. And only God Himself can free you from a yoke (contract). For example, a man can easily soul-tie himself to a woman, and they'll enter a boyfriend/girlfriend agreement, whereas either spoken or implied, both parties are expected to be faithful to one another, spend time together, respect one another, or whatever else they've agreed to do and be for another. But a girlfriend can't sue her boyfriend or his lover for cheating on her; the same is true for a boyfriend. He can't sue his girlfriend for cheating on him. They have little to no legal rights in the natural or the spiritual realm. However, a husband is yoked to his wife. He can estrange himself from her, but until he divorces her (legally), he will remain legally bound to her. And yes, a boyfriend can yoke himself to his girlfriend (and vice versa) by getting her to live with him, make promises to him, and enter into agreements and contracts with him, such as buying, renting or leasing a house. Or she can yoke herself to him by buying or leasing a car, getting a joint bank account, starting a business together, etc. Consider 1 Corinthians 7:39, which reads, "The wife is bound by the law as long as her husband liveth; but if her husband be dead, she is at liberty to be married to whom she will; only in the Lord." The Greek word for "bound" in this text is "déō," and according to Thayer's, it means:

1. to bind tie, fasten

    a. to bind, fasten with chains, to throw into chains

    b. metaph.

2. Satan is said to bind a woman bent together by means of a demon, as his messenger, taking

possession of the woman and preventing her from standing upright

3. to bind, put under obligation, of the law, duty etc.

 b. to be bound to one, a wife, a husband

4. to forbid, prohibit, declare to be illicit

Matthew 19:6 reads, "Wherefore they are no more twain, but one flesh. What therefore <u>God</u> hath joined together, let not man put asunder." This has often been a heated debate in the Christian community. Can a woman remarry after she's been divorced? Here are a few keys:

1. A wife is bound by the LAW as long as her husband lives.

2. What God has brought together, no man is to divide or put asunder. We all know that most marriages today were not brought together by God, but this still doesn't give us the clearance to marry and divorce people whenever we please.

3. The most commonly used scripture regarding this matter is Matthew 19:3-10, which reads, "The Pharisees also came unto him, tempting him, and saying unto him, Is it lawful for a man to put away his wife for every cause? And he answered and

said unto them, Have ye not read, that he which made them at the beginning made them male and female, and said, For this cause shall a man leave father and mother, and shall cleave to his wife: and they twain shall be one flesh? Wherefore they are no more twain, but one flesh. What therefore God hath joined together, let not man put asunder. They say unto him, Why did Moses then command to give a writing of divorcement, and to put her away? He saith unto them, Moses because of the hardness of your hearts suffered you to put away your wives: but from the beginning it was not so. And I say unto you, Whosoever shall put away his wife, except it be for fornication, and shall marry another, committeth adultery: and whoso marrieth her which is put away doth commit adultery."

Notice in the aforementioned text, Jesus said:
1. Whosoever shall PUT AWAY his wife, except it be for fornication, and MARRY another commits adultery.
2. Whosoever MARRIETH a woman who has been PUT

AWAY commits adultery.

Why didn't He say, "Whoever divorces his wife and marries another," or "Whoever marries a woman who is divorced?" The simple answer is the words "divorce" and "put away" are not the same. Do your research! Back in those days, some men would have a change of heart just as humans tend to do today, and they wanted to divorce their wives, but they had no moral grounds to do so. During that era, a man's name was his credit; it opened doors or shut doors in not just his life, but in the lives of his parents, siblings, wife, children, grandchildren, and for generations to come. Men could divorce their wives by giving them a writing of divorcement for various reasons, but divorcing a woman simply because you've grown weary of her was sorely frowned upon. To the Israelites, this screamed that the man in question was not a man of his word because he was dishonoring his word to his wife's father. He was dishonoring and disregarding the ketubah; this was a marriage contract that grooms made with their father-in-laws regarding their commitments to their newfound wives. All the same, the men paid a huge bride price to get their wives. It could take them years to fully fulfill a bride price, and believe it or not, many (if not most) fathers would give the wealth they'd accumulated from the bride price to their daughters. So, the wealth would go from the husband to the father, and then to the husband-to-be's potential bride. She would come into the marriage with all of those possessions. If a man were to divorce his wife for any reason outside of sexual immorality, he would have to return every bit of the bride's price back to her. He would have humiliated his father, offended his father-in-law, and sent a message to the whole Jewish community that he was not trustworthy. To a Jewish man, doing this would be worse than death itself! So, many men elected to put away their wives instead of divorcing them. In this, they would continue to honor their obligation of providing for and protecting their wives. But because the woman had not been given a writing of divorcement, she was still married; the same was true for her husband. They were still legally bound to one another, so it was illegal for them to marry other people.

The Bible tells us to not be unequally yoked with unbelievers. The word "yoke" here is a legal term, and it comes from the Greek word "zugos," and according to Strong's Exhaustive Concordance, it means, "from the root of zeugnumi (to join, especially by a "yoke"); a coupling, i.e. (figuratively) servitude (a law or obligation); also (literally) the beam of the balance (as connecting the scales) -- pair of balances, yoke." In this, God is telling us to not enter into any legal agreements, including marriage, with unbelievers. But what if you did just that? What if you married an unbeliever when you were an unbeliever, or what if the closer you've gotten to God, the further you've gotten away from your spouse? Apostle Paul gave the church a set of instructions to abide by. 1 Corinthians 7:10-15 reads, "And unto the married I command, yet not I, but the Lord, Let not the wife depart from her husband: But and if she depart, let her remain unmarried or be reconciled to her husband: and let not the husband put away his wife. But to the rest speak I, not the Lord: If any brother hath a wife that believeth not, and she be pleased to dwell with him, let him not put her away. And the woman which hath an husband that believeth not, and if he be pleased to dwell with her, let her not leave him. For the unbelieving husband is sanctified by the wife, and the unbelieving wife is sanctified by the husband: else were your children unclean; but now are they holy. But if the unbelieving depart, let him depart. A brother or a sister is not under bondage in such cases: but God hath called us to peace."

So, what can we take from these scriptures?

1. The Lord hates divorce.
2. There is a difference between being divorced versus being separated (put away).
3. Separated equals still married!
4. A husband can divorce his wife and a wife can divorce her husband for sexual immorality (adultery and other sexual crimes).
5. Apostle Paul recommends that if a woman is married to an unbelieving husband or a man is married to an unbelieving wife, and the unbelieving spouse desires to remain married to the believer, the believer should remain in the marriage and attempt to win the unbeliever's soul. Peter instructed in 1 Peter 3:1-2, "Likewise, ye wives, be in subjection to your own husbands; that, if any obey not the word, they also may without the word be won by the conversation of

the wives; while they behold your chaste
conversation coupled with fear."

This is to say that if you leave a marriage illegally, the
yoke still stands! This is why we should always pray,
seek wise counsel, and fast before making such a life-
altering decision. This is also why it is imperative that
all believers pray and search the scriptures before
adopting anyone's interpretation of the scriptures
(including my own). Your job is to seek God for yourself,
otherwise you can easily find yourself bound by religion,
all the while having a third-party relationship with God
through your pastor or your favorite social media
personality. 2 Timothy 2:15 states, "Study to shew
thyself approved unto God, a workman that needeth not
to be ashamed, rightly dividing the word of truth."

Note: here's an experiment I often give people to help
them understand marriage, soul ties, and divorce. Grab a
cup, go to the kitchen sink, and fill that cup up halfway
with water. After you're done, grab one of your favorite
bottled waters, open it up, and pour some of it into the
cup. Wait for two minutes. Now grab two more cups, and
I want you to separate the hydrant water from the

bottled water in the cup. This is an impossibility, right? Of course, it is! There is no scientist, marine biologist, water technician, hydrologist, engineer, or entity outside of God Himself who could perform this feat! This is what it looks like to separate two souls, especially souls that have been brought together by God. Only God can fully break a soul tie, and only God can destroy a yoke, and He does this using His anointing. "And it shall come to pass in that day, that his burden shall be taken away from off thy shoulder, and his yoke from off thy neck, and the yoke shall be destroyed because of the anointing" (Isaiah 10:27).

CLEAVING VS. CLINGING

> Therefore shall a man leave his father and his mother, and shall cleave unto his wife: and they shall be one flesh.
> Genesis 2:24

Have you ever been around someone who is incredibly clingy? I'm talking about a person who will not go a day without text, calling, or showing up at your house? I'm talking about a person who is insecure about almost everyone in your life? I'm talking about a person who appears to be emotionally unhinged whenever you tell them that you're busy, you're tired, or when you say no to them. Yes, it's likely that the individual in question is infected with the spirit of Jezebel, and at the same time, that person has an inability to cleave, and that's why they cling. When a person is clingy, that individual will be relatively controlling (often passively), incredibly insecure, and envious. Now, you might not see the envy materializing itself in the beginning, because they will mask it with gifts and flattery, but over the course of time, you will start to notice them mimicking some of

95

your quirks, habits, commonly used phrases, and your overall style. This is because the individual has lost his or her identity a long time ago, and they have decided that they like your identity. Please note that people try on personalities every day. Why do you think that the movie industry's revenue is over $70 billion a year, and is projected to go over $100 billion?! People are sheep; that's not a degrading statement, that's biblical. As humans, we tend to shop for traits, quirks, and characteristics that appear to produce the results that we want to have. So, we may pick up a lip-biting habit from one actress, a seductive squint from another actress, a cute facial expression from another actress, the confidence that another actress portrayed, and so on. Over time, we tend to lose ourselves in an attempt to find love, remain relevant, and avoid rejection altogether. But what's ironic is, the more we lose ourselves, the more we lose our abilities to cleave, thus causing us to become clingy.

What's the difference between cleaving and clinging? The following definitions were taken from Merriam Webster:

- **Cleave:** to adhere firmly and closely or loyally and unwaveringly.
- **Cling:** to hold or hold on tightly or tenaciously; to have a strong emotional attachment or dependence.

In simplistic terms, to cleave is to be connected by God, but to cling is to be connected to something or someone you revere as a god. This is why Mark 10:9 says, "What therefore God hath joined together, let not man put asunder." To cling is to be in idolatry. It means to be soul-tied or connected by another thread other than God. We need soul ties to cleave, just as we need them to cling, and of course, soul ties can be good just as they can be evil. They can work for you or against you. They can work for your flesh and against your purpose; this is why so many of the relationships that God calls us out of didn't initially appear to be bad relationships. We may have had amazing friendships with people, only for God to confuse our language with those people because what we were building with them did not give Him glory. Understand these truths:

1. You can be soul-tied to people who aren't soul-

tied to you.

2. You can be best friends with someone who is not your friend at all.

3. A person can be a friend of your perversion, but an enemy of your purpose.

4. A person can be a scab on a wound that you have, but when you heal, he or she will fall away.

5. Your best friend in one dimension can be your worst enemy in another.

The Bible tells us that God is all-knowing. This is why we should always pray before building relationships with people, and we should also pray before promoting people in our lives. We can accidentally promote someone out of purpose and into a space in our lives that God hasn't carved out for them. For example, you can promote your closest friend from being your friend to being your best friend, and almost immediately, a set of problems will begin to arise in your relationship that weren't there before. Why is this? It may have something to do with your definition of a best friend or your friend's definition of what it means to be besties. For many people today, the terms "friends" and "best friends" come with a list of expectations, some good, while others are binding and unrealistic. People will plug you into roles that were created by pain, neglect, rejection, trauma, and ignorance, and the minute you accept those roles in their lives, your relationship with them will begin to fail and falter. This is because you're now sitting on an altar in that person's heart that God is out to destroy or you may have that person in a space in your life that is reserved for God. Therefore, after you've transition that individual from one place to another, you may find that what was once your closest friend is now behaving like she's your boyfriend or husband. She may start becoming more controlling, more needy, more demanding, and more insecure. This is because you have now connected yourself to a space in her life where there is an incredible void. As a reminder, all voids are God-sized, and cannot be filled by humans, material items, or money. Some of them have to be filled by God, while others have to be destroyed.

To better understand the difference between a cleave and a cling, grab a roll of tape. Cut off a small piece of that tape and stick it to your arm. You'll notice that when you do this, it will adhere or stick to your arm pretty firmly. Now, take the tape off your arm and look at it. You should see oil and debris on the tape, albeit, very lightly. Stick the tape back to your arm. What do you notice? It's not as strong as it was initially. This is because you've just used its ability to cleave, and now, you're entering the cling. In other words, it was not designed to be laid down and pulled back up to be used again. And the more you stick it to your skin, and then remove it, the less adherence it will have. To get the same or similar strength from that tape, you will have to wrap it around your arms several times. This is an unhealthy adherence; this is what a cling looks like. It looks like you holding onto someone who God has instructed you to let go of. It looks like you holding onto someone who isn't interested in you. It looks like you settling for someone who thinks they're settling for you. But only what God brings together forms a cleave, and that's not just in romantic relationships, it can be found in platonic, professional, ministerial, and every type of relationship there is. However, the most sacred cleave is the one we form with God, and the second most sacred one is the one we form with our spouses.

The Greek word for "cleave" is "proskollaó," and according to the Lexicon, it means, "To join closely, to cleave to, to adhere to." This implies proximity, after all, it is illegal to be closer to your mother than you are to your spouse. Beware of people who:

- ✓ Move too fast in relationships.
- ✓ Demand a greater proximity to your heart than your parents or children when they are not yet married to you.
- ✓ Are always accusing you of cheating on them or sneaking around behind their back when you're being faithful to them.
- ✓ Get incredibly upset whenever you don't answer their phone calls or when you don't answer it as fast as they want you to answer it.
- ✓ Have routine meltdowns because of their fear of losing you, only to come back and apologize again and again without changing their behavior.
- ✓ Demand excessive amounts of your time, so much so that it begins to affect you in the workplace, your mental health, and your other close-knit relationships.
- ✓ Do weird things like sniff your clothes, place

tracking devices on your vehicle or question your every move.

✓ Threaten to commit suicide if you were to break up with them or put space, time, and distance between the two of you.

✓ Do not respect your boundaries. (Note: Only bound people hate boundaries.)

✓ Tend to hold onto their former connections with exes, old friends, and toxic people out of fear that they'll eventually need those people again.

Those souls are not unhealed, and they will make your life a living hell if you tolerate them. They don't have the ability to cleave because they're still cleaving to someone else or something else. And like the python spirit, they will suffocate you until it begins to affect you relationally, mentally, emotionally, financially, spiritually, etc. I've had clingy people in every area of my life, and every last one of those relationships fell apart. This is because the soul ties formed in those relationships slowly but surely become chains, and there's no way to kindly break free from bondage.

- **Matthew 11:12:** And from the days of John the

Baptist until now the kingdom of heaven suffereth violence, and the violent take it by force.

- **Hebrew 12:4:** Ye have not yet resisted unto blood, striving against sin.

In closing, we can lose our ability to cleave when we attach ourselves to the wrong people, or we can weaken our ability to connect with people in a healthy way. This is what science refers to as an "anxious attachment style." Positive Psychology reports the following information regarding anxious attachment styles:

"Also known as anxious-ambivalent or simply "anxious attachment style," anxious-preoccupied attachment manifests as an intense need for constant reassurance and validation from others, stemming from early experiences of inconsistent care-giving and emotional hunger.

Children raised in environments where caregivers were unpredictable in their responsiveness or emotionally unavailable may internalize a deep-seated fear of abandonment and rejection.

In childhood, individuals with this attachment

style may exhibit clingy behavior, constantly
seeking attention and approval from caregivers.
In adult relationships, they may become overly
dependent on their partners for validation and
reassurance, often feeling overwhelmed by fears
of rejection and exhibiting jealousy or
possessiveness."

(Source: PositivePsychology.com/Anxious Attachment
Style: What It Is (+ Its Hidden Strengths)/ Laura Copely,
Ph.D.)

Remember, earlier we discussed what a void is. It is a
black hole in the soul, and it has a gravitational pull
called attraction. This attraction goes far beyond a
desire to connect with or get closer to a person. It
becomes a stomach of sorts, whereas broken souls tend
to fill themselves with the time, resources, and the souls
of other broken souls. And that's why you'll never be
enough for them, because there's no way you or any
other person can fill that void. Consequently, these
people will eat you up and spit you out repeatedly until
you lose your grit. "Have all the workers of iniquity no
knowledge? Who eat up my people as they eat bread, and

call not upon the LORD" (Psalm 14:4).

It's simple. We have to heal. And no matter what we do, we can't cleave to someone God didn't call us to, and we cannot use clingy behaviors as an alternative for cleaving. If we cleave to the Father, allow Him to heal us, mature us, and fill our voids with His presence, He will restore our ability to connect firmly and healthily to the right people. In other words, we will establish Godly soul ties, as opposed to cutting our hair, getting face-lifts, or altering our bodies altogether in an attempt to get someone who has no ability to cleave to form an unholy bond with us. You're better than that! When God wants to connect you with someone, He will do it on His terms and in the right season, but when you do it yourself, you will always connect to the wrong people in the wrong way, or you'll connect to the right people in the wrong season and totally destroy that relationship before it is set to begin. Choose wisely.

Multifaceted, Multidimensional & Multi-Talented

> But we all, with open face beholding as in a glass the glory of the Lord, are changed into the same image from glory to glory, even as by the Spirit of the Lord.
>
> 2 Corinthians 3:18

According to Cambridge Dictionary, the word "multifaceted" means "having many different parts or sides." We are made in the image and likeness of God, and understand this—God is multidimensional, multifaceted, and multi-gifted. In truth, He embodies it all—every gift, every talent, and every good thing. James 1:17 confirms this; it reads, "Every good and perfect gift is from above, coming down from the Father of the heavenly lights, who does not change like shifting shadows."

What does it mean to be multifaceted? Simply put, it means to have many faces or many sides. I want you to imagine yourself as a spinning wheel, with faces all around. When people meet and form a relationship with you, they will spin you around and talk to the side of you that they can relate to. In this, you have the following faces:

Parental	Daughter/Son	Romantic
Professional	Platonic	Familial
Biblical/Faith	Financial	Cultural
Selfish	Educational	Spiritual

Most, if not all, of these faces correlate to the Greek understanding of love; for example, Agape is God's kind of love, Storge means family love, Philia means the love of a friend, Eros represents romantic love, etc. Howbeit, these are the many faces or sides of the human. And what you'll notice is that every person who has access to you or tries to gain access to you is pulling on one or more of your many facets or faces. Some people will talk to you for hours on end about family matters. You cannot venture outside of the topic of family without them getting bored. If you were to spin around and start talking to them about faith, you will notice that they will start to appear disinterested. This is because they don't like, agree with, or desire to communicate with that side of you, OR that particular side of them is dark. And when I say "dark," I don't necessarily mean that they are evil; I mean that there is no revelation on that side of them. They have little to no knowledge, for example, about money, so to them it may be embarrassing to discuss money matters with you. This is especially true if you are highly knowledgeable about money, how it works, and how to manage it. So, if you were to start a conversation with them about money, they may give you a quick answer, change the topic, excuse themselves from your presence, or start to focus on other things like their cellphones, their children, the people around them, etc. Then again, some people may allow you to communicate with that side of them when they are struggling financially because they are hoping to get some tips or some money from you.

Understand this—the word "void" means "a completely empty space," according to Oxford Languages. It means to be unoccupied, desolate, or when dealing with matters of the mind or soul, it means to be ignorant. The word "ignorant" comes from the word "ignore." It means that information is present, but you choose to ignore that information in favor of other information or in favor of being entertained. Therefore, a void is a black hole in the soul; it is an empty space. According to 1 John 1:5, "This then is the message which we have heard of him, and declare unto you, that God is light, and in him is no darkness at all." What does light do? It illuminates a space; this illumination is called revelation. It means to reveal. Every face that we have represents a space or realm in our souls, and in those spaces, there are principles. Principles are the seats of principalities or ruling spirits. If you have Godly principles in your financial state, and you apply those principles, revelation will fill that space, and the evidence of that revelation will show up in your money. People will see you begin to prosper financially because in that room, you are able to see what God has placed on the inside of you. After all, Heaven is not up. According to the scriptures, Heaven resides within us (see Luke 17:21). And when that space is filled with revelation, you'll be proud to show it off to others. However, if you show that side of you to someone who is void or dark in the area of finances, that person will turn into a human vacuum. You see, a void is a black hole in the soul, and it has a gravitational pull called attraction. This is why people who live in poverty are so intrigued and attracted to people who are prosperous. This is also why a lot of wealthy people will not form close connections with impoverished people. In most cases, this has nothing to do with them exalting themselves above the poor. It has everything to do with their own personal encounters and experiences. They soon learned that someone who has a void in the financial realm could easily depend on them, idolize them, and exploit them, and in some cases, maybe even try to rob or kill them to get access to their money. Remember that it is the love of money that is the root of ALL evil. So, many wealthy people tend to create programs designed to teach people how to acquire wealth; they do this to help others and to protect themselves because wealth makes them a target for broke or, better yet, broken people. To be broke is to be broken. It doesn't mean that the individual in question is bad; it simply means that the individual has not yet been made whole. This is to say that whenever people try to connect with you, they are often interested in one of your many sides or faces. It is imperative to pay attention to what side each individual repeatedly pulls on. For example, let's say that you are on the ministry team at your church. You're always praying for people, casting out demons, and counseling people. Howbeit, there is another girl on the ministry team who you've caught looking at you in the most sinister way. And every time she engages with you in conversation, she pulls on your platonic side, but here's the problem—you are not interested in being her friend because you've already seen how jealous-hearted, insecure, and double-minded she is.

The platonic state is an intimate state; it is a space that rests pretty close to your heart, and yes, this is the same heart that God told you to guard. In this, you can clearly see her intentions. Because she's jealous of you, she feels threatened by you; consequently, she's determined to study you up close. So, the door she's chosen is the entrance way for friends-only. To avoid her creating the soul tie with you that she wants to create, your job would be to spin around and repeatedly address her using the side of yourself that you don't mind her having access to. I would respond by repeatedly engaging her in professional talks, but not so much about entrepreneurship. Instead, I'd be speaking about our roles at the church in a professional way. If she tried to speak about someone at the church in a degrading way, I'd say, "Let's pray for her right quick." The objective here is to diligently guard your heart because an attempted connection by the wrong person or the wrong people is the foreshadowing of a demonic attack. Or whenever you find that you have connected with someone in the wrong way, which has led to a lot of foolishness, barrenness, or wasted time, your best outlet is to spin around; this means to repent and to get back on course. A great example is—Fred has been friends with Jason for three years, and recently, he's discovered that Jason is using him for money. This seems like an easy resolve, but here's the kicker—Fred is confident that God connected him with Jason, and every time he prays about the situation, he feels that God is telling him to stay connected to Jason. What Fred has to do is breakup with Jason platonically. One prayer I like to pray is, "Lord, don't let me connect with (insert name here) in the way that I think I should be connected with her, and don't let (insert name here) connect with me in the way she wants to connect with me. Instead, give me the role in her life that you've called me to have, and give her only the roles in my life that you've called her to have." Of course, I seal my prayer with "in Jesus' name," and then I relax from there. What God has taught me is to stop defining my relationships; He's taught me to stop telling my relationships what they are, and to let them define themselves. This way, I don't end up becoming friends with someone who reveres me as their competition, their enemy, or the mother they wished they'd had. Your relationships will declare themselves! What you'll find is that the woman you thought you'd become best friends with is only equipped to be your friend, your sister in Christ, or someone you're mentoring. Then again, the other woman you wanted to be close friends with may prove to be your big sister in Christ, and had you put the wrong label on that relationship, you would have made it difficult, if not impossible, for her to pour into you. Please note that many of your relationships that have failed over the years weren't necessarily demonic relationships; they were simply relationships that you put the wrong labels on.

Just like we are multifaceted, we are also multidimensional. The word "dimension" is defined by Oxford Languages as, "a measurable extent of some kind, such as length, breadth, depth, or height." Let's talk depths and heights. Just like you have many sides to you, each side of you has a depth and a height. For example, some people will repeatedly have surface-level conversations with you about certain matters. Let's use the financial side of you. Consider Myron Golden. He is a public speaker, a business growth consultant, a best-selling author, and a financial strategist. He is a powerhouse and a bank of revelation as it relates to money matters. If you were to come face-to-face with Mr. Golden, and you had a surface-level measure of knowledge about money, you wouldn't be able to say much in that conversation with him. In this, you have to recognize that you can't be the teacher; you have to see yourself as a student if you want to become wiser. This means that you'd have to close your mouth and open your ears, only opening your mouth to ask questions. I tell people all the time that it is a dangerous and foolish thing to repeatedly sit at tables where you do more speaking than you do listening. You need to sit at tables that you don't feel qualified to sit at; this way, you can learn more instead of competing for a spot in a conversation with a bunch of folks who are in your zip code of revelation. In this, none of you are feeding each other! You're simply waiting for your turn to add to the conversation, and when you get your turn, you're speaking loudly and passionately in an attempt to keep your friends from cutting you off every time you say something that stirs, offends, or inspires them. So, if you were seated at a table with Myron Golden, you wouldn't have much to contribute to the conversation, but if you allowed your pride to take a front-row seat, you'd likely over-talk the man, say some of the most foolish things while using "big words," and you'd run him off. Remember, deep calls onto deep (see Psalm 42:7), so if you're not that deep on that particular side, your best response should be silence, taking notes, smiling, a subtle nod of the head, and a few "wows" here and there to let him know that you are listening and that you're interested in the conversation. You may, on the other hand, have a friend who, in the financial realm, is a surface-level theorist, and whenever the two of you talk about money, entrepreneurship, and your plans to acquire wealth, you tend to laugh, tell stories, and paint your fantasies for your friend to see. This isn't bad at all; it will serve to encourage and inspire you, but you want to have teachers in the realm where you are empty, dark, and void of knowledge, wisdom, and understanding. You don't want to have a bunch of classmates and students with no teacher, otherwise, every person on that side of you will only serve to entertain you. Then again, you might not be that deep. Understand that depth comes from digging, so the goal is to start getting knowledge, but above knowledge acquisition, be sure to get understanding. Understanding is as it sounds; it goes into the depth of knowledge to excavate wisdom.

- **Proverbs 4:7:** Wisdom is the principal thing; therefore get wisdom: and with all thy getting get understanding.
- **1 Corinthians 8:1:** Now as touching things offered unto idols, we know that we all have knowledge. Knowledge puffeth up, but charity edifieth.

People will often try to soul-tie themselves to the side of you that they favor. Some people will try to tie themselves to the side of you that they envy. This is so they can study and mimic you. Also, there are people who will seek to soul-tie themselves to the stickiest part of your soul, and that is the side or sides of you that you haven't yet adhered to the Word of God. For example, a narcissist will look for your voids. This is because a narcissist is an individual who is bound by the Jezebel spirit, and Jezebel loves idol worshipers. Wherever you're ignorant is the same space that you're godless or polytheistic, meaning you haven't fully made a decision as to whom you will serve in that region. You may declare Jesus as your Lord and Savior, but your lord is not who you claim, it's who you serve. That's how the spirit realm works. You can't claim a lord that you refuse to serve. This is why Jesus said in Luke 6:46, "And why call ye me, Lord, Lord, and do not the things which I say?" Also, consider these scriptures:

- **Matthew 15:8:** This people draweth nigh unto me with their mouth, and honoureth me with their lips; but their heart is far from me.
- **Matthew 7:21-23:** Not every one that saith unto

me, Lord, Lord, shall enter into the kingdom of heaven; but he that doeth the will of my Father which is in heaven. Many will say to me in that day, Lord, Lord, have we not prophesied in thy name? And in thy name have cast out devils? And in thy name done many wonderful works? And then will I profess unto them, I never knew you: depart from me, ye that work iniquity.

Again, Jezebel, the narcissist, will seek to connect themselves with you in the area that is void of God. Sure, you can meet a religious narcissist at church, and he or she may use the scriptures to get you to lower your guard, but this isn't necessarily how the narcissist wants to connect with you. Instead, Jezebel will use your fears, insecurities, ignorance, father/mother wounds, or idolatrous ways as a means to connect with you, and they will try to solidify and legalize the soul tie through sexual sin. And they can and will try to do this dimensionally as well. So, if you meet a false shepherd disguising himself as a man of God, and he uses the Bible, his title, and your ignorance as it relates to the things of God to gain access to you, he may begin to dig a ditch in your soul. Another word for "ditch" is "trench." BibleHub reported the following from Topical Encyclopedia:

> "**Military Use:** Trenches were commonly used in ancient warfare as defensive structures. They provided protection for soldiers and were often part of a larger fortification system. In 2 Kings 3:16, the prophet Elisha instructs the Israelites to dig trenches in the valley as a divine strategy against the Moabites: "This is what the LORD says: 'Make this valley full of ditches.'" . These trenches were miraculously filled with water, confusing the Moabite army and leading to Israel's victory. This account highlights the strategic importance of trenches in military operations and the belief in divine intervention in battle.
>
> **Agricultural Use:** In agricultural settings, trenches were used for irrigation and drainage, essential for sustaining crops in the arid climate of the region. The practice of digging trenches for water management is implied in various biblical narratives, though not always explicitly mentioned. The use of trenches in agriculture

underscores the dependence on water and the ingenuity required to cultivate the land effectively.

Religious and Ritual Use: In religious contexts, trenches were sometimes used in sacrificial rituals. A significant example is found in the account of Elijah on Mount Carmel. In 1 Kings 18:32-35, Elijah challenges the prophets of Baal and prepares an altar to the Lord. He instructs the people to dig a trench around the altar: "And with the stones, he built an altar in the name of the LORD. Then he dug a trench around the altar large enough to hold two seahs of seed. Next, he arranged the wood, cut up the bull, placed it on the wood, and said, 'Fill four jars with water and pour it on the offering and on the wood.' 'Do it a second time,' he said, and they did it a second time. 'Do it a third time,' he said, and they did it a third time. So the water ran down around the altar and even filled the trench."

This trench served a dual purpose: it demonstrated the power of God when the water-soaked sacrifice was consumed by fire, and it symbolized the separation of the holy from the profane."

(Source: BibleHub.com/ Trench/ Topical Encyclopedia).

This is to say that the trench or low place provides a false sense of protection, provision, and priesthood which, ironically enough, are the three dimensions of a husband. He is to be the protector, provider, and priest of his family. What does the Bible say about these types of leaders? In Matthew 15:14, Jesus warned us this way: "Let them alone: they be blind leaders of the blind. And if the blind lead the blind, both shall fall into the ditch."

One of the deepest levels and most sacred spaces of the soul is our faith. Sure, we have a side of us specifically dedicated to our faith, but every side of us has a foundation; this is where our foundational beliefs reside, and this is where our faith is located. In short, each side of you will be filled with information, and the information that we retain becomes knowledge if we believe in that information. Most of this information comes together to form theories, beliefs, and principles.

- **Theory:** These are a set of loose-fitting beliefs that come together to form what we call "hunches" or ideas. We tend to have surface-level theories, just as we often have theories that are deeply set.

- **Beliefs:** This is the information that we've accepted to be truths or facts. What differentiates them from principles is that a belief can stand alone, and while it may affect other beliefs and theories that we have, many beliefs don't have enough weight or information to back them for proper implementation into certain areas of our lives. Consequently, they become silent beliefs that we may share with the people who are closest to us, but they don't necessarily drive our other beliefs or affect all or most of our choices.

- **Principles:** Oxford Languages defines the word "principle" this way: "a fundamental truth or proposition that serves as the foundation for a system of belief or behavior or for a chain of reasoning." Principles are the skeletons of our belief systems. They affect every part of our lives. For example, we believe that Jesus Christ is Lord, He is the Son of God, He was a perfect man who came into the Earth over two-thousand years ago, was crucified and killed, rose on the third day after His death, and He now sits on the right hand of God making intercession for us. He is the Messiah. Because we believe these truths, we also believe that murder is wrong, fornication is wrong, God is love, prayer is our way of communicating with God, etc. This is because the Bible is a series of stories and truths that are interconnected; we can't believe a part of the Bible and then reject other parts of it. Sure, some Christians attempt to do just that—they pick and choose which parts of the Bible they want to believe, but let me submit this to you. These people don't know God because God is the Word, and they are rejecting the Word in favor of a group of words. In other words, they want a paragraph of Jesus, but they don't want the full story, and you can't dismember the Lord. " He keepeth all his bones: not one of them is broken" (Psalm 34:20). In this, the foundation of who Jesus is, both in body and in spirit, cannot and will never be split apart. Another way of saying this is—facts (the flesh) can never be separated from the truth (the foundation/bones), and the truth cannot be bent or broken. The moment the truth is stretched or a set of facts point you away from the truth, the statement ceases to be true; instead, it is a well-crafted lie. This is why Galatians 5:9 reads, "A little leaven leaveneth the whole lump." One lie can pervert a statement and render it untrue.

Again, the point is—you are a multifaceted creature, and every side of you has depths, heights, and widths. The depth of each side is determined by the depth of Word study you've put in, and how much of that revelation you've accepted into our life as a core belief. The height of each side has everything to do with how much you've ascended in Christ by seeking the face of God. This has everything to do with your face-time with God. The width of each side has everything to do with sacrifice;

this has more to do with how much you've journeyed with Christ or how far you've gone for the gospel of Jesus Christ. For example, consider the life of Abram turned Abraham. He journeyed on foot and in heart to follow God, electing to walk by faith and not by sight. Or what about Moses who forsook his power and position as the step-grandson of Pharaoh to lead God's people out of Egypt and into the Promised Land? Then, there's Joseph who was thrust from his place of comfort, sold into slavery, where he found himself in Potiphar's house fighting off the whelms of Potiphar's lustful wife. After this, he found himself in prison serving time for a crime he didn't commit, and ultimately, he found himself in his purpose, standing next to Pharaoh. Now, these three men traveled on foot, however, we don't necessarily have to travel physically unless God instructed us to. We do have to pursue God through Bible study and prayer, and some of us are called to go deeper than others because of the call of God that is on our lives. In other words, a standard Bible study won't do! We have to go deep into the Word through in-depth study, prayer, and through serving leaders who God has paired us with. We don't have the luxury of being "normal" or "comfortable." Instead, we had to learn to find comfort in discomfort until we learned to embrace our Comforter.

So, remember that there are many faces that you have, and each person you come in contact with is going to pull on one or more of those facets of you. Pay attention to the side, depth, and height of you that they pull on the most. It will tell you how they perceive you, what role they want you to fill in their lives, and where they stand in their walks with Christ.

And finally, most of us are gifted. Notice that I didn't sell you the idea (just to be nice) that every believer is gifted. After all, the Bible does not proclaim this. Don't get me wrong; God gives gifts to His children, but that's not what I'm talking about. I'm talking about being gifted. 1 Corinthians 12:1-11 reads, "Now concerning spiritual gifts, brethren, I would not have you ignorant. Ye know that ye were Gentiles, carried away unto these dumb idols, even as ye were led. Wherefore I give you to understand, that no man speaking by the Spirit of God calleth Jesus accursed: and that no man can say that

Jesus is the Lord, but by the Holy Ghost. Now there are diversities of gifts, but the same Spirit. And there are differences in administrations, but the same Lord. And there are diversities of operations, but it is the same God which worketh all in all. But the manifestation of the Spirit is given to every man to profit withal. For to one is given by the Spirit the word of wisdom; to another the word of knowledge by the same Spirit; to another faith by the same Spirit; to another the gifts of healing by the same Spirit; to another the working of miracles; to another prophecy; to another discerning of spirits; to another divers kinds of tongues; to another the interpretation of tongues: but all these worketh that one and the selfsame Spirit, dividing to every man severally as he will."

Obviously, there is a difference between being talented versus being gifted. What is the difference? A gift is an inherent ability that you were born with, but a talent is a natural ability given to you by God to do a thing. An example of a gift would be the supernatural ability to play a musical instrument masterfully with little to no practice after hearing it one time, but an example of a talent would be someone else's ability to play that same instrument through practice, dedication, and hard work. We are born with gifts, but talents are given to us. Consider the parable of the talents. Matthew 25:14-30 tells the story; it reads, "or the kingdom of heaven is as a man traveling into a far country, who called his own servants, and delivered unto them his goods. And unto one he gave five talents, to another two, and to another one; to every man according to his several ability; and straightway took his journey.

Then he that had received the five talents went and traded with the same, and made them other five talents. And likewise he that had received two, he also gained other two. But he that had received one went and digged in the earth, and hid his lord's money. After a long time the lord of those servants cometh, and reckoneth with them. And so he that had received five talents came and brought other five talents, saying, Lord, thou deliveredst unto me five talents: behold, I have gained beside them five talents more. His lord said unto him, Well done, thou good and faithful servant: thou hast been faithful over a few things, I will make thee ruler over many things: enter thou into the joy of thy lord. He also that had received two talents came and said, Lord, thou deliveredst unto me two talents: behold, I have gained two other talents beside them. His lord said unto him, Well done, good and faithful servant; thou hast been faithful over a few things, I will make thee ruler over many things: enter thou into the joy of thy lord. Then he which had received the one talent came and said, Lord, I knew thee that thou art an hard man, reaping where thou hast not sown, and gathering where thou hast not strawed: And I was afraid, and went and hid thy talent in the earth: lo, there thou hast that is thine. His lord answered and said unto him, Thou wicked and slothful servant, thou knewest that I reap where I sowed not, and gather where I have not strawed: Thou oughtest therefore to have put my money to the exchangers, and then at my coming I should have received mine own with usury. Take therefore the talent from him, and give it unto him which hath ten talents. For unto every one that hath shall be given, and he shall have abundance: but from him that hath not shall be taken away even that which he hath. And cast ye the unprofitable servant into outer darkness: there shall be weeping and gnashing of teeth."

Each servant had been handed or given talents, and each of them made the decision to either use their talents or bury them. The unfaithful servant decided to be slothful, narcissistic, and spiteful, as we can see in the text. We can also see that none of the servants had the same amount of talents or abilities; this had everything to do with their measures of faith. Faith leads to faithfulness, but we can have faith in God, we can have faith in ourselves, or we can have faith in others. Whomever gets our faith gets our faithfulness. So, while you are multifaceted, there are some sides of you that have talents, and some people will seek to soul-tie themselves to those sides of you so that they can benefit from your talents. For example, when I started creating websites and logos for ministries around 2007, I learned a lesson that had to embed itself in me, and that lesson was—there are a lot of ungodly leaders out there. That lesson had to dig its way into my heart, and it caused me many tears, howbeit, I also learned that there are a lot of Godly and amazing leaders out there. The ultimate message I got from this was that I had no choice but to look at the fruits that each leader bore, instead of looking at the titles, the miracles performed by them, the number of people that follow them, etc. I had to learn to stop being surface-leveled and superficial. This is because I had leaders galore trying to "son" or "daughter" me in their attempts to get free graphic design work. Most graphic designers who've worked with ministries have experienced this. These leaders simply have a wrongful relationship with their money, and because of this, they've become cunning, manipulative, and rebellious. I've worked with over a thousand ministries over the years, so I've dodged many lassoing attempts. Nevertheless, I'm grateful for those experiences because they taught me a lot of invaluable lessons; they also set the stage for my faith to grow because I came to see that the Word of God was, is, and will forever be truth. I'm sharing this to say that your talents will attract people to you, both good and bad, just as your gifts will make room for you and bring you before great men (see Proverbs 18:16). Your job is to try the spirit by the Spirit (see 1 John 5:1), and again, pray about everyone and everything. Last, but certainly not least, let each relationship define itself over time. Ask yourself the following questions:

1. When my friends call me, what side of me do they

pull on the most?

2. When my parents call me, what side of me do they pull on the most?

3. When my significant or insignificant other engages me in conversation, which side of me do they love to meet with the most?

Do this with everyone in your life, and also pay attention to the depth, height, and width of each interaction. Look at patterned-conversations. In other words, pay attention to the topics that the individual in question keeps returning to or leading you to. Or look for their style of conversation. Does the conversation always end in them talking about someone in general? Does the conversation always end in them talking about different people? Does the conversation always find its way to talks of men, marriage, and failed relationship attempts? And pay attention to the height, depth, and width of each conversation. I have people in my life who, anytime we speak, stay on the surface, but our conversations are good. I also have people who, whenever we do speak, engage with me on a deeper level. I have people who love to have carnal (not sinful) conversations with me; then again, I have people in my life who love to have spiritual conversations with me. So, get this, if I don't want to be deep on any given day, I'm probably not going to call my deep friends. The same is true for the carnal folks. If I don't want to have surface-level conversations on any given day, I will likely avoid the people who may be young in the faith or people who are having carnal experiences that they want to talk excessively about. For example, Alfred may want to talk to me about his aunt's live-in boyfriend and how the guy called him questioning who he was. I may have discovered that most of Alfred's conversations are about his over-the-top experiences in life, and they are always just above the surface (carnal). Because of this, I'll likely avoid Alfred on days when I just want to get lost in the presence of God all day, talk deeply about spiritual things, and engage in in-depth dialogue about the Bible with another believer. If Alfred's phone number shows up on my caller-ID, I'm probably going to send the guy to voicemail. I'd follow it up with a text message saying that I'm busy and asking him a single question: "What's up?" That's a kind way of asking, "What do you want?" Alfred may text me back, letting me know that he got his haircut at a different barber than the one he ordinarily uses, and the guy butchered his hair. There's nothing bad about this conversation, but it's more surface-level, and again, if I don't want to have any small-talk on that day, I won't let Alfred spin me around to the side of me that he wants to engage, and then proceed to have a surface-level conversation with me because my mind will wander off while he's talking to me, and I may fall asleep, start scrolling the internet, or I may become (in his opinion) overly spiritual. He may want to stay on the surface, but I'd say something along the lines of, "You know, according to the Bible, your hair is your glory. This may be a sign that you need to find a different barber. To me, this shouts jealousy. I know it might not be that deep, but if this is a pattern of his, you may want to consider getting a new barber, and be sure to ask God to send you to the person He trusts with your crown." In this, Alfred may become offended or thrown off because he wanted to speak reproachfully about the guy or share a moment of laughter, but instead, he called the wrong person on the right day. He called me when I could feel the tangible presence of God, and instead of allowing him to bring me "back to Earth," I took the dude into the deep and drowned him in revelation. Consequently, Alfred would likely get off the phone with me, call a carnally-minded family member, and talk about his latest encounter with me. Then again, he may take to social media and post something along the lines of, "Some people are so deep that they forget to come up for air. Relax, saints! You won't go to hell if you spend one night on Earth!"

This is simply to say that we are multidimensional, multifaceted, and multi-talented people every single day of the week, and if you don't want to be surrounded by the wrong people, your saving grace is being who you authentically are everyday. Your authority is found in your authenticity. Sure, it's both okay and advisable to "meet" people where they are, but don't let them keep you there. When you visit people in a realm of thought that's lower than the realm you exist in, YOUR GOAL IS MINISTRY. If you meet them there platonically, they will create soul ties with you that are designed to keep you where they are, and if the devil gets involved, he'll try to find a way to get you to yoke yourself to someone in that dimension. This is done through marriage, partnerships, agreements, etc. This way, you'll forsake or limit the call of God on your life in favor of friendship, marriage (to the wrong person), power through collaboration, etc. Read this carefully—there are a LOT of major gifts out there who've married minor-minded people; consequently, their ministries, businesses, and alliances did not reach their full potential. I've met and ministered to many men and women of God who can't even write a book without their spouses acting out or acting up. Every time they sit down to write, their spouses' demons manifest themselves; they start fights, start talking about divorce, and some of them become violent. This is because God gives us helpmates, but Satan strategically hands out hindrances if you go within a realm of thought that God has brought you out of and you start forming the wrong types of relationships in those realms.

FROM TALKS TO TIES

Pay attention to the depth of your conversations and
how they make you feel. Also pay attention to the point
behind each dialogue because statements without
conclusions often set the stage for confusion. You don't
necessarily need an immediate conclusion, but you do
need to study the matter out so you won't have too much
unaccounted for information sitting in the waiting room
of your mind. And I'm not saying to consciously dissect
every conversation or interaction while you're having it,
after all, that would ruin the moment. Instead, it is good
to reflect back from time-to-time so that you can get a
general idea of the other party's perspective of you, the
side of you that they love to engage, and the depth of
conversation they like to engage you in.

Last but not least, pay attention to the length of any
given conversation. What did the two of you talk about

the most? What were you most interested in? What was the other party most interested in? Understand this—when the enemy brings or sends someone into your life for the sake of binding, delaying, hindering, perverting, or rerouting you, that person will have a favorite side of you, and they will repeatedly spin you around so that they can engage that side of you. This is likely because there's a void on that side. In other words, you are ignorant in that realm, and wherever there is ignorance, there is the potential for idolatry. What this would signal is that the enemy is trying to soul-tie you to that person in that particular realm. For example, let's say that you are a single woman and you have formed several non-romantic relationships with a few of the guys at your church. All of these guys have girlfriends and female interests, so you don't have much of a relationship with them outside of a hello and a hug in passing. However, a few of them have your phone number, and whenever they do call you, it's typically about issues at the church. Let's give these guys names. There's Craig, Luke, and Patrick. Craig is a complainer. Anytime he calls you, he's complaining about something or someone. He just needs a listening ear. He's single, but he's never had a single conversation with you about love, dating, marriage or the like. Luke, on the other hand, is in a full-blown relationship. As a matter of fact, he's been romantically tied to Natalie for the last three years. Whenever Luke calls you, he calls to ask you questions about entrepreneurship and all-things money related. However, he always changes the subject mid-conversation. His pattern is, he'll wait for you to say something that he can use as an entryway into the matter that's really pressing his mind: Natalie. He may say, for example, "Yeah, I like what you said there—you have to be faithful and consistent if you want to succeed in business. That's so true. It's like that in every world. That's what I was telling Natalie the other day. I said to her, 'Nat, you can't repeatedly show up for everyone else, and then when the man who chose you wants to spend time with you, he has to wait in line. If you do that, all of your other relationships will thrive at the expense of this one. That's what I don't understand about some women. They say they want a good man, but when they get one, they don't know how to treat him.'" What's happening here is—Luke didn't want to talk about business, but he was too embarrassed or too prideful to lead with the conversation he really wanted to have, so he decided to feel you out first. One of three things is true about your relationship with Luke:

1. He respects you and sees you as a wise counselor, but he's too embarrassed or prideful to admit this.

2. He's trying to turn you into a sidechick (you'll know if this is true if he starts asking questions like, "Would you do that to your boyfriend if you were in this situation?" or "I was thinking to myself (insert your name here) wouldn't do that to me if we were dating. Am I right?")

3. He's frustrated and doesn't know where to turn, so he's talking to everyone who'll listen about Natalie.

So, what you've noticed was that he called and pulled on the entrepreneur in you, and then after he started engaging you on that side, he spun you around and started engaging another side of you, which is fine— it's what people do from time-to-time. However, if you notice that this is Luke's pattern, your goal should be to find out why Luke keeps talking about relational matters with you. What's his objective?

And let's not forget about Patrick. Patrick is always dating someone at the church or interested in someone at the church, and every time he calls you, like Luke, he starts off engaging one side of you, and then he spins you around and starts talking about women, relationships, and marriage. He presents himself as the ideal husband—the good guy who can't seem to find a good woman in the grand sea of women in the Earth. "I'm with you," he says. "I know that God is going to choose the right one for me because every time I choose someone, I end up ghosted, cheated on, or emasculated." Here's the truth about Patrick:

1. His self-esteem is low, so he uses your encouragement, compliments, and advice to recharge himself between relationships.

2. He's arrogant. Don't get it confused—you can have low self-esteem and still be arrogant, conceited and cocky. You see, self-esteem has to do with what you know about yourself, your abilities, your faith, and your superpowers. Confidence, on the other hand, has everything to do with who you confide in, who you allow to confide in you, and what you're relying on. It's incredibly common to

143

come across cocky and conceited people who have low self-esteem; that's why they'll easily sleep with a married person or they will allow people to use them and then discard them. Patrick's arrogance has everything to do with a fact—the fact is, he's not bad on the eyes and he's come to realize that women are drawn to him visually. Howbeit, the truth of the matter is—he's broken in other areas, so his skin has become his mask.

3. You might be his ideal woman mentally, morally, and spiritually, but you might not be his ideal woman aesthetically. I've witnessed this many times. I remember ministering to a young woman who kept showing up for a guy who used her to help build his business, launch his ministry, and to discuss the matters of his heart. He talked to her excessively about relationships, his career goals, and money matters. She said that the two of them were a perfect match, however, he showed no interest in her romantically. She complained that they would speak for hours on end, and he'd confirmed to her time after time that he loved her personality, her money-mind, and just her mind in

general. He called her everyday. He involved her in every matter of his ministry and work life. He opened his heart to her, sharing with her his most intimate plans and secrets. When she reached out to me, she was confused. She believed that she was the perfect woman for him, but when she'd finally chanced it and spoke with him about them building a relationship together, he shot her down by saying that she was his sister in Christ— nothing more. He then proceeded with the relationship that they'd built. He consulted with her about every love interest he had, used her to help build, brand, and launch his business and his ministry, etc. I made it plain and clear for her. She was his sidechick, even when he didn't have a woman. I told her that she was everything that he wanted inwardly, but visually, she wasn't his type, even though she was beautiful. I remember it dawned on me while speaking with her—he didn't want a black woman. Yes, he was a black man, but he didn't want a black woman. We were mid-conversation when this download came in, so I told her. She gasped. "Tiffany, you're right! He only dates white women! The woman that he's dating and complaining about now is white!" Of course, I told her to cut ties with the guy and stop letting him use her for supply. In the world of psychology, supply is the attention, validation, admiration, and praise that narcissistic people need to feed their grandiose views of themselves.

Again, when the enemy brings or sends someone into your life to bind, delay, hinder, pervert, or redirect you, that person will have a favorite side of you, and they will repeatedly spin you around so that they can engage that side of you. That's the face of yours that he or she likes the most. And if the individual in question is demonized, narcissistic, or if he or she has ulterior motives, they will find the side of you where you are ignorant, insecure, or arrogant. For example, let's say that you are a guy, and on the world's beauty scale, you clear an easy four or five. In other words, you're considered to be average-looking, at most. You don't get a lot of female attention, but you have had your fair share of women who were interested in you. One day, you meet a woman (we'll call her Jane), and based on the world's scale, Jane rates about an eight or a nine. She's an incredibly beautiful woman on the outside, but inwardly, Jane is hideous. Jane knows that on the carnal scale, she is out of your league, but intellectually and spiritually, you're way out of her league. What you'll notice is that when speaking with Jane, she will steer away from certain sides of you, especially those sides of you where you're rich with revelation and filled with confidence. Jane would spin you around to address the side of you that has to do with your physicality, because in this realm, she feels superior to you, and in this realm, she believes that she can lord herself over you by making you feel like you're unworthy of her time and attention. So, if I were advising you, I'd tell you to cut ties with Jane. Remember these words—never tolerate someone who attacks your self-esteem or your self-worth. When I was a teenager, I had a friend who kept saying that I had big ears. She made me believe that my ears were large and they stuck out. Neither of these assertions were true. I tolerated her for years on end, and she worked tirelessly to break my confidence. Why? Because I got a lot of male attention, and I was confident (sometimes even cocky) enough to terminate a relationship that wasn't healthy. She was beautiful, but she lacked confidence; her self-esteem was incredibly low, and I'd worked overtime to help her build it, telling her how pretty she was, pointing out the guys who'd tripped over their own shadows while looking at her, and helping her to find clothes that complimented her. Nevertheless, that child wanted to destroy every ounce of my confidence. And for years, I felt insecure about my ears, often hiding them with hairstyles designed to cover them up. That was until when I was around 19-years old, I started wearing ponytails and other styles that pulled my hair away from my face. I then noticed that my ears don't stick out at all, and they aren't big. They are average-sized! I told my other friends, and everyone looked at me in dismay. "Girl, you don't have big ears," they'd shout as they bobbed their heads from side-to-side to get a better look at my ears. And just like that, my confidence was restored, but it taught me a valuable lesson—one that I still live by to this day nearly thirty years later—do not give people with low self-esteem access to your heart or mind. Anyone who comes after your self-worth and confidence is an enemy of your purpose! Don't get me wrong—I love engaging with people who tell me, for example, "That hairstyle doesn't do you justice," or "That outfit isn't for your body type. Let me show you a few outfits I think will look good on you." Notice here that the person in the example is giving me a solution, not just a problem. All the same, if the individual gets upset because I may not like the clothes or styles they are suggesting, I won't listen to them at all because they are manifesting a spirit of control. However, if they say, "No worries, how about this outfit?" while sending me photos of other styles, I know that the person's intentions are good.

Satan loves to use conversations to set the stage for soul ties to form, and he is strategic as it relates to where and how those ties are formed. This is why no conversation is "innocent." It may be innocent on your end, but you don't fully know the goal or intentions of the person you're engaging with. Sure, they may start the conversation on one side, and then spin you around when you least expect it and begin to form a relationship and soul tie with you on another side.

How do you block someone from spinning you around and forming an ungodly, unhealthy, and demonic soul tie with you?

1. Don't give everyone your number. Nowadays, it is best to give them your Instagram handle and let them reach out to you on there.

2. Pray before you give anyone access to you, and be sure to wait until you get a clearance from God before you exchange numbers with them.

3. When someone is communicating with you, and they try to spin you around to engage a broken, undeveloped, or unhealed part of you, spin back around and engage them on the side that they started with. For example, if Ramona is trying tirelessly to become your friend and she keeps calling you to talk about school, and then she keeps trying to take an exit in the conversation into talks of family, men, and people in general, grey-rock her in that realm, and then spin back around. To grey-rock someone means to ignore anything they've said that was designed to get a negative, emotional, or detailed response from you. Your goal is to show low to no interest in the conversation they want to have, to disengage them in the areas where they are trying to engage you. So, if Ramona tried to pull a fast one and go

from being my schoolmate to my friend, and I don't want to be her friend because she's proven herself to be messy, I would laugh and say, "Okay," anytime she tried to change the subject or I'd say, "Yeah, that's crazy. Did you finish your sociology assignment? I'm almost done with mine." Or I wouldn't entertain or engage the question at all. Why? Because Ramona is trying to create a soul tie or a bridge of sorts between my soul and her soul, and I don't want what's in her to have access to my heart. In other words, I'm guarding my heart against what I may sense or see in her, or I'm guarding my heart until I can sense and see what's in her.

4. Tell the truth and shame the devil! Be honest with people. I may, for example, say to Ramona, "Hey Ramona, I think you're a nice lady and I love speaking with you, but right now, I don't want to get too personal with you. I want to focus on my education with no distractions, and I appreciate you trying to get to know me on a personal level, but I don't want to open that door just yet because I want to remain focused in this season. I

hope you understand."

5. When someone repeatedly tries to spin you around, even after you've grey-rocked them or communicated your boundaries with them, cut that person off. Only bound people hate boundaries.

Remember, what seems like an innocent conversation can lead you to form soul ties with unhinged or ungodly people. A soul tie formed with a toxic, ungodly, narcissistic, or double-minded person is not just a soul tie—it's a chain, and it's designed to bind, limit, and hinder you. Resist the chains of oppression and learn how to form the right types of bonds with the people in your life.

DIRECTIONAL SOUL TIES

> For what is a man profited, if he shall gain the whole world, and lose his own soul? Or what shall a man give in exchange for his soul?
> Matthew 16:26

There are different types of soul ties; the same is true as it relates to lengths and strengths of ties. I know it may sound like I'm reaching, but after you read this chapter, I am confident that you'll understand what I mean.

As a reminder, the soul is comprised of the mind, will, and emotions. The mind is what the Bible refers to as the heart; this is what God told us to guard. This is the black-box, control center, and engine of the soul, and anything that gets access to your heart has a measure of control over your life. It is for this reason that Satan sends his devils after you. No, he won't necessarily come after you himself because Satan is not omnipresent. He cannot be in more than one place at a time, but he does have representatives, and those representatives are known as devils, also known as demons. The goal of a demon is to oppose the will of God; that's it and that's all. Like their father, the devil, they come to kill, steal, and destroy. But demons understand something that a lot of humans don't understand, and that is—legalities. For example, I had a dream around 2009 or 2010, and I was in a foreign country standing in the middle of a narrow road talking to three women. To the left and right of us were rolling hills, but it felt deserted. Nevertheless, we were all happy. The three women were facing me, and I was facing them. I was talking to them, and I remember that they were all smiling and receiving whatever it was that I was sharing. They appeared to be elated; that is until something behind me caught their attention. They all started looking down as if they were not allowed to make eye contact with whomever it was that was behind me, so I turned my head and noticed a dark-complexioned male wearing sunglasses approaching us. I didn't recognize the guy while I was asleep, but when I woke up, I recognized him. I'd never truly engaged this guy outside of giving him a fake number back when I was unsaved, and he'd run into me at my job. There, he'd confronted me about giving him a fake number, and I pretended that he'd remembered it incorrectly (at that time, cell phones weren't a thing. If we didn't have pen and paper handy, we had to memorize numbers, which is what he'd attempted to do). I asked him what number he'd called, and once he quoted it, I'd said, "Oh, that's the problem. My number isn't 334, it's 332." Embarrassed and relieved, he'd apologized to me, and from that day on out, I made it a point to hide whenever I saw that guy out in public. But now, some twenty-odd years later, there I was dreaming about the guy, and obviously, in my dream, he wasn't a good guy. He'd walked up to the first woman on my left, entered her personal space, and then took her phone out of her hand. She didn't resist. She didn't say a word. She just kept her head down. He then repeated this crime with the woman in the center, and again, she didn't fight back or say a thing. Afterwards, he walked over to the girl on my right, and entered her personal space, took her phone, and watched to see if she'd respond. There was silence. And finally, he turned around to face me, but I wasn't avoiding eye contact with him, even though he was wearing sunglasses. I was confused. Why were the women letting him take their phones away, and why were they afraid of him? He wasn't that tall of a guy; he was probably around 5'7. We could all take him if we banned together. My thoughts were all over the place, and it goes without saying that he reached into my hand and snatched my phone. I then begin to challenge him. I don't remember exactly what I said, but it was in the area of, "How dare you take my phone! I'm calling the police!" He was taken aback, but his facial expression didn't change. "You're going to call the cops on me, huh?" he asked in an eerily calm tone. "Yes, I'm calling the police!" I exclaimed. He then nodded his head in a slow, methodical way. I called the cops, and that's when the dream transitioned to me seeing him standing on that same narrow road talking to the cops. They were standing outside of their police car, but I was surprised that they hadn't arrested him. Instead, I stood there stunned as the cops handed the guy a set of what appeared to be court documents, and after this, they left. Once they were gone, the guy started walking towards me at a slow pace, but I took off running. I ran from house to house, but everyone would invite me into their homes because they agreed with my stance, but once the news would come that he was on his way there to come and get me, they'd put me out. After this, I woke up. I won't give a full interpretation of the dream, but in this, God was showing me a part of my assignment. I would be speaking to women and helping them to recover what the enemy stole from them (their voices), but first, I'd have to recover what he'd stolen from me: my voice. What do you do on a cell phone? You talk on it, right? That's the main reason for it. Him taking their phones represented him taking their voices, and just as he'd taken their voices, he'd taken mine, but I took mine back. I then called the cops. Calling the cops in dreams represents prayer, and whenever you see a (good) cop in your dreams, that cop likely represents an angel of God. And angels are the enforcers of legalities. What did they hand the guy in question? A set of legal documents. But the problem was—I ran for a season. Years later, I would have a similar dream, whereas I was in the custody of that same man, along with a few other women, but he trusted me. He didn't trust me because I was serving him (I wasn't), he trusted me because he'd held me in captivity so long that he was convinced that I'd go run an errand for him and return out of fear and familiarity. Spoiler alert: I ran away. I ended up going into a bank and hiding behind the counter. I explained to the cashier what had just happened, and she called the cops for me. This represents intercession. The wicked man came in the bank looking for me, but the cashier pretended as if she didn't know where I was. Not long after this, I remember looking out the huge windows of the bank and seeing him in handcuffs. He looked at me while wearing those dark sunglasses as I watched him be taken away by cops. His season in my life had ended because I'd chosen to pray and I refused to remain in captivity. I was more determined to be free than he was to hold me in bondage. That's the key to deliverance! If the devil is more passionate about holding onto you than you are about getting free, you will remain in captivity to him.

Notice in both dreams, the cops showed up. Think naturally. A cop has to have a legal right to arrest you, otherwise they will have to free you because the courts would rule that your detention is unlawful. And in order for a cop to show up, you have to call them (in most cases) or someone has to call them on your behalf. All the same, you have to press charges against your offender. Please remember these words—demons are always looking for a legal right to bind you, however, they sometimes bind people illegally, and when they do, they can easily be cast out. The ones who use their legal rights to bind and hold a person will hold up their legalities when addressed. This is why, before deliverance, the people who want to be free have to repent and renounce whatever it is that the devil is holding on to, and in many cases, they have to fast.

The women in the first dream were obviously intimidated by the guy, so they lowered their heads to show their submission to him. They had the appearance of freedom, after all, we were outside on a long road surrounded by green pastures, but they weren't free at all. They were bound souls who the devil had let out for recess. It was obvious that the guy (demon) had some type of hold on them, and that hold happened to be fear. Fear is one of the many soul binders that we are going to discuss later on in this book. But first, let's talk about directional soul ties. They are:

1. Two-way soul ties.
2. One-sided soul ties.
3. One-dimensional soul ties.
4. Multifaceted/Multidimensional soul ties.
5. Phantom soul ties.
6. Massive (or mass) soul ties.

7. Third-party soul ties.

Two-Way Soul Ties

These are your standard soul ties connecting one person to another person. For example, if Zachary started dating Dana, they would likely form a two-way soul tie with one another through communication and association. It's also important to note that soul ties aren't always sexual or ungodly. They start their formation when we begin to open our hearts, oftentimes through sharing intimate details about our lives to another person. They also form when we share space, time, and resources with people. Soul ties are often founded on trust; they can also be established on distrust, trauma, and shared experiences, both good and bad. Most two-way soul ties aren't actually bilateral, given the fact that we often soul-tie ourselves to other people, and then, we soul-tie ourselves to our present partners, bringing the unsevered soul ties with us. This creates a highway of soul ties, and that highway allows for a lot of demonic traffic, confusion, and issues.

One-Sided Soul Ties

Yes, you can soul tie yourself to someone who isn't soul tied to you. One-sided soul ties are often formed when we invest more time, resources, and effort into an individual who's invested little to no time, resources, or effort into us. All the same, you can form one-sided soul ties with your favorite celebrities and influencers. In this, you can come to care about someone who doesn't even know you exist. Now, this doesn't make them bad people, after all, someone with a thousand followers will find it nearly impossible to get to know all of his followers, let alone someone with 10,000 followers, 25,000 followers, 100,000 followers, or millions of followers. This is to say that some one-sided soul ties can be beneficial, especially when what's coming through the soul tie is the Word of God, encouragement, and revelation. However, some are toxic—especially the ones where a man or woman, for example, will have a lot of interest in someone who is not interested in them. And regardless of what the other person says, the interested party can form a belief about the other party, and this could lead to obsession. Obsession is a demonic soul tie; it happens when a rejected and unhealed soul doesn't cast down the imaginations that the enemy plagues him or her with and forms an unhealthy relationship with the man or woman in their minds. They will then come to believe that the object of their affection possesses certain qualities —these qualities are the traits that they imagined those people to have while fantasizing about them, and these qualities are oftentimes what they believe they need to live a healed and whole life.

One-Dimensional Soul Ties

Remember, we are multifaceted creatures, meaning we have many sides to us. And whenever people show interest in us, they are often interested in one or more sides. All the same, they aren't necessarily interested in us per-se; they are typically interested in our mindsets or our physical bodies. So, you might meet, for example, a guy named Tony, and while Tony is incredibly attracted to you physically, physical attraction isn't enough to sustain a relationship. So, if Tony is truly interested in getting to know you, he's going to look for a section or a group of principles that you have that align with the principles that govern his life. That is, once again, if he wants to have a true relationship with you. If he wants

162

to have a physical relationship with you, he won't care if you're highly intelligent or chronically incoherent, his only objective will be to get you out of your clothes.

One-dimensional soul ties involve people soul-tying themselves to one dimension or facet of a person. For example, most women have dated men who were only physically attracted to them, but were not interested in their thought-life, desires, plans, or fears. Most men have dated women who were only financially attracted to them, but were not interested in their thought-life, desires, physique, plans, or fears. This is what a one-dimensional soul tie looks like. And it goes without saying that these types of relationships don't last long because it is hard to live life on one side. In other words, it is difficult to be with someone who emphasizes one side of you, all the while leaving the other sides neglected. I imagine that if you did this with a jewelry stand, it would rust and become hard to turn. This is one of the reasons that whenever we leave relationships where only one or a few sides of us were entertained and emphasized, we often feel free enough to say, "I'm finding myself" because we are! We are finding the pieces of ourselves that we've shelved for months and, in most, cases, years.

Multifaceted/Multidimensional Soul Ties

This one is self-explanatory. Again, we have multiple sides of us, and the people who come into our lives will typically find the sides of us that they want to soul tie themselves with, just as they will find the sides of us that they want to avoid at all costs. And yes, there will be people who are interested in multiple sides of us, and they will soul tie themselves to every one of those sides. To make this plain, let's create a character. Dorothy meets a guy named Floyd, and she's attracted to Floyd's face, his love for God, his workplace ethic, his business acumen, and his sense of fashion. Floyd is an articulate man, debonair even, who appears to be the perfect man to most women. Howbeit, there is a problem in paradise. You see, whatever areas of a person you are attracted to is the area where you are building a soul tie in. So, Dorothy has managed to tie herself to Floyd in many ways, but Floyd has this one issue that Dorothy loathes. In times past, she's even referred to this issue as a deal-breaker. The issue is—Floyd is big on family; keeping his family together is a huge priority to him, and this would be an invaluable trait to have if Floyd's family members weren't so toxic and narcissistic. He allows his mother to show up at his house unannounced, and she's always treating him like a child, controlling every aspect of his life. She even inserts herself into Dorothy's relationship with Floyd, and Floyd often writes off her behavior as her being overly protective of him. This is to say that Floyd's mother has stolen his cleave in the parental dimension; this is a torch that was supposed to be passed to the romantic realm. Consequently, while Floyd and Dorothy are soul-tied to one another in so many ways, they will form the wrong type of connection in the Eros realm because Floyd's mother has stolen his heart.

This is simply to say that we can soul-tie or connect ourselves to other people in many ways, and if the enemy comes to destroy that relationship, he will break each tie one-by-one, starting with the stronger ones. He'll do this principle by principle and line by line until the soul tie breaks, we break up, or we have a breakdown and become broken.

Phantom Soul Ties

These imaginary soul ties are but a figment of the imagination. It's when we come to believe that this or that person is the one for us. You see, the heart has to be unguarded to receive love. Love can be given by one party, but it has to be accepted by the other. So, one of Satan's favorite attacks today is to disguise himself as an angel of light, and connect certain people together. You may find yourself just walking around your neighborhood one day, when all of a sudden, you see what appears to be the most beautiful man in the world. And without warning, you hear, "That's your Kingdom spouse." If you're not careful, you'll form a phantom soul tie with the person, and you'll read into everything they do or say. So, if the person looks at you for too long, you'll come home, plop down on your couch, and go into a state of euphoria, mentally rewinding the moment when your eyes met. The other party may be totally oblivious to the attack you're under, and may think that you're weird or socially awkward. Howbeit, you'd come to believe that the other party likes you, is in love with you, and wants to be with you, and you'll excuse their lack of pursuit with:

- "He's shy."
- "He's afraid I'll reject him."
- "God showed me that he's still praying about me."

In this, you may formulate an actual soul tie with the individual in question, but he or she won't be soul-tied to you. All the same, you may formulate a soul tie based on who you think your love interest is. In other words, you can't love what and who you don't know, so if you imagine a person having traits, and it is those traits that you end up falling in love with, you will tie yourself to a phantom: a figment of your imagination.

Massive or Mass Soul Ties

Soul ties don't break just because you've broken up with a person or vice versa. No, most people are walking around this Earth soul-tied to an ex of theirs (or multiple exes). Media and culture encourages the world to go out there and date everyone they're interested in, so promiscuity has become normalized in certain communities and families. Consequently, the dating pool is nothing but a cesspool filled with fractured souls looking to "connect" themselves with other people. The problem is that they are still cleaving and clinging to the folks from their pasts, and the folks from their pasts are still clinging to the folks from their pasts. This creates a huge bed of sorts, whereas those who practice fornication are really a part of a mass, worldwide orgy. And it is for this reason that:

- 41% of first-time marriages end in divorce.
- 60% of second marriages end in divorce.
- 73% of third marriages end in divorce.

Consider this. A man (let's call him Chad) meets and marries the woman of his dreams (let's call her Debbie), and at first, all is well. He's happy, content, and excited about building a future with her. However, he's still soul-tied to Keisha, Karen, Nancy, and 37 other women. Those women are soul-tied to over 500 men, and those 500 men are soul-tied to over 40,000 women who are soul-tied to 350,000 men. This creates a freeway for demons and demonic activity. If COVID didn't teach us anything, it should have taught us that the world at large is connected. This is to say that the world is a part of a system; they are a part of a massive soul tie. This truth even reigns true for believers who are still a part of the world and believers who are unequally yoked with unbelievers. What travels to Chad will travel to and through Debbie, and eventually, it'll make its way from North America and find itself on the continents of Africa, Asia, Europe, South America, Australia, and maybe even Antarctica should they break up. This is why the Bible warns us against fornication. It herds people into one bed, spiritually speaking, and causes them to switch partners every time they switch relationships.

Third-Party Soul Ties

These soul ties are formed when outside voices become a part of a relationship, and those voices become the strings that are holding those relationships together. A great example of this is the relationship that Jacob had with Rachel. He had to go through her father to form and legalize marriage to her, and even after they got married, Laban (Rachel and Leah's father) still monitored and controlled his son-in-law. That is until Jacob decided to break free and take his wives and children with him.

Third-party soul ties are often soul ties formed with or through a middleman. For example, think about the infamous, meddling mother-in-law who controls and manipulates her son so much that his wife begins to feel unprotected, unwanted, and alone. The mother-in-law in question may encourage her daughter-in-law to get closer to her, confide in her all the more, and bring all of her marriage matters to her. In this, the mother-in-law has the title of sorts to her son's soul, and in order for the guy's wife to have a decent enough relationship with her husband, she would have to go through his mother. This means that he's cleaving to his mother while clinging to his wife, and over time, he will drop his wife trying to hold onto his mother.

Third-party soul ties can also include debtors, since "the rich ruleth over the poor, and the borrower is servant to the lender" (see Proverbs 22:7). Get this —financial problems are said to be the catalyst behind 20-40 percent of divorces. This is why God told us in Romans 13:8, "Owe no one anything, except to love each other, for the one who loves another has fulfilled the law." It is difficult to cleave to someone who's working overtime because their master is demanding more time and attention than you are.

What about lengths and strengths of soul ties? You can

have a longstanding soul tie with a person; yes, even if you haven't spoken with that individual in years. For example, an ex of mine tried and pursue me around 2015; we had dated some 20 years prior. He'd said to me, "I never fell out of love with you. I thought about you everyday," or something along those lines. He was still soul-tied to a version of me that no longer existed, and I told him this. "She's dead and gone," I said, "And she won't be resurrected." He wasn't a spiritual person. He referred to God as "the man upstairs," and said that he didn't attend church, even though he believed in God. I had one conversation with him, and immediately knew that God hadn't sent him. Howbeit, I utilized the three days that I spoke with him over the phone to let him know that none of it was real. The old Tiffany could not love anyone; she was incredibly prideful, self-centered, narcissistic, and broken. As a matter of fact, I didn't even try to love anyone. I reasoned within myself that I was just having fun, and if I met the right man while doing so, que será, será. But the Tiffany he had reached out to was a new creature in Christ who'd divorced and slaughtered the old Tiffany with the Sword of Truth. Howbeit, he found it hard to believe this. Before I ended

171

our communications, I'd shouted, "I break that witchcraft off you in the name of Jesus!" He was surprised. "You put witchcraft on me?" he asked. "No, not traditional witchcraft," I said. "I never got into that, but I seduced you—intentionally." He was confused. "So, what you're saying is what we had wasn't real?" I didn't waste any time to respond, "No, it wasn't. I was a seductress. You felt how I wanted you to feel; that's how I was back then, and seduction is a branch or form of witchcraft." I'm sharing this to say that the old me was the third-party in that soul tie, and I felt the need to break it off of him, or at least try to set him free from it. He'd been bound by an ungodly soul tie to a phantom; he'd been holding onto who I'd become, not who I am. Therefore, he was caught up in a phantom soul tie, and the length of that soul tie spanned over 20 years. He'd boasted about lying next to his wife and thinking about me over the years. Of course, I wasn't flattered; I was sorrowful because he was in the process of going through a divorce. I learned in that hour that many marriages are destroyed because one or both of the people in those marriages are still soul-tied to another person or their perception of another person.

And the length of a soul tie isn't just limited to or
associated with time. It is also associated with borders
and boundaries. Let me explain. I have a course called
Remnant Writers, where I teach Christian authors how to
write books. I used to actively teach the course between
2016 and 2019, but now, it's available for replay. One of
the warnings I gave each class that I taught was
this—once you start stepping into your purpose, any
demon that still has access to you internally or
externally will likely try to resurface. So, beware of any
exes that suddenly reappear while you're writing your
books; the enemy (likely) sent them to stop you from
writing. It's a legality. Revelation 12:11 states, "And
they overcame him by the blood of the Lamb, and by the
word of their testimony; and they loved not their lives
unto the death." We overcome the enemy by the blood of
the Lamb, along with the word of our testimony. When
we're testifying about our lives, our pasts, and our
hangups, we are simultaneously putting the devil on
blast, and he won't stand for this if he can do anything
about it. Nevertheless, despite my many warnings, I have
witnessed a few students get ensnared by the "return of
the unclean spirit" while writing. The problem was—they

became flattered, instead of seeing their exes' reemergence for what it was—a demonic attack. Of course, they'd told me in the beginning that their exes had suddenly contacted them, like I'd warned, but after this, they started keeping quiet about their dealings with these dudes. And in 100 percent of those cases, those ladies did *not* finish their books, even though my class had a 98% success rate.

This is what I call a soul leash. Think about a dog's leash. Some people tie their dogs to poles and trees using four, six, eight, and ten-foot leashes, and while I don't agree with this type of pet-parenting, it still happens. But each pet can only go as far as his or her leash allows. Remember, in my second dream about the evil man who'd kidnapped me and a few women, he'd gotten to a space where he trusted me to run errands. He let me out one time, and I used that opportunity to go on the run. Like a dog chained to a tree, I had once been chained to a demonic altar, and whenever I started wandering around in church, the enemy didn't mind because I was still serving that altar. He trusted me to fail, he trusted me to fall, he trusted me to return to my vomit, but over time, I learned to trust God. What I've witnessed with myself and others over the years is this—whenever someone is chained to an altar or bound by a demonic agreement, they will be on a leash and/or a lease. They can do so much and go so far before Satan starts pulling on their leashes or holding up their leases. Some people have more legroom than others because the enemy trusts them; this is especially true when he possesses whatever it is or whomever it is that they idolize. This is when the devil has become their dealer. What the men and women who'd taken my Remnant Writers' class witnessed was how strategic demons are. Many of them had exes who suddenly reappeared, but only a few of them were ensnared by those exes. The rest took my advice, ignored the exes, and continued to write their books until completion.

You see, what happens is, whenever you start to do and be what God created you to do and be, hell will typically send out a set of devils to come and retrieve you. They want you to stay within the bounds of whatever limits they've set for you. And they will almost always send people who you are familiar with, or they'll send new love interests if you're too guarded as it relates to your exes. When you're on a leash or a lease, Satan can feel

175

you tugging on that leash, and like any good pet owner, he will start pulling you back towards himself or back within the limitations and boundaries he's set for you. In this, he may let you attend a great church for years; he'll let you praise God, shout, dance, run laps around the sanctuary, and do back flips in the church, but the minute you try to get on the ministry team, or the moment you start writing the book God told you to write, getting therapy, going deeper into the Word of God, starting a business, going back to school, he'll feel that tug of the leash. From there, you may begin to experience warfare; this warfare includes:

1. Family members acting out.
2. Exes attempting to return.
3. Current boyfriends/girlfriends acting out or ending the relationship.
4. Talks of divorce between you and your spouse.
5. Job loss.
6. Money problems.
7. New potential love interests trying to enter your life.

These are just satanic attempts to pull on your leash and hold up your lease. The way to break this is through repentance, submitting yourself to God, therapy, and going through deliverance. All the same, you must do what God instructed you to do and stop obeying the warfare.

Lastly, let's talk about the strength of a soul tie. Most of us have experienced loving someone far more than we've ever loved another person. In truth, it likely wasn't true love, but we had heightened feelings, great expectations, and more respect for some of our past lovers. For example, I remember the first and only time I'd ever experienced obsession. I was 17-years old and I'd just experienced heartbreak for the first time in my life. I'd allowed myself to become obsessed with the man I'd just broken up with, and that obsession led me to declare to all of my friends that I would break up with any guy I was dating if that man reappeared in my life and wanted to reconcile our relationship. Yes, I was bound! This is to say that the soul tie I had with him was far stronger than the soul ties I'd experienced with any man before him. Simply put, some people have a greater hold on their lovers, friends, and spouses than others. Then again, a strong soul tie isn't always romantically-centered. Some people have stronger soul ties with their parents than they do with their spouses. Some people have stronger soul ties with their lovers than they do with their children. Some people have stronger soul ties with themselves than they have with anyone; this undoubtedly is called selfishness and narcissism.

The point is—not all soul ties are equal. Some are young, some are old; some are strong, some are weak; some are one-sided, while others are multidimensional. However, they can be broken by the power of God. You just have to remember that breaking a soul tie isn't an event where you light candles and chant a set of words; again, the church has to get delivered from being witchcraft-minded when it comes to the power of God. Breaking a soul tie requires repentance, meaning you have to return to your first love: YAHWEH. And your return can't be a visit or a series of visits. You have to take up residency in His heart, otherwise, Satan will use his lease or his leash to drag you back into the darkness and back into the very soul tie that he's using to strangle your potential.

HAREMS VS. HOUSES

> And he had seven hundred wives, princesses, and three
> hundred concubines: and his wives turned away his heart.
> 1 Kings 11:3

Polygamy still exists, but it hides behind the
girlfriend/boyfriend mask. Polytheism still exists, but it
hides behind the "God knows my heart" tagline.

Let's start with the word "girlfriend." This term can be
traced back to the late 19th century, specifically around
the 1890s. The term is a combination of the words "girl"
and "friend," both of which have deeper linguistic roots.
The word "girl" initially referred not just to a young
female but also to a young person of either gender until
the late 15th century. As for "friend," it hails from the
Old English "freond," which means "to love." Amazingly
enough, the concept of friendship has always been
intertwined with affection and tenderness.

However, during the 19th century, the meaning began to
narrow. As romantic relationships became more

formalized, the word "girlfriend" emerged as a term to describe a girl who was more than just a friend—a girl with whom one had a romantic relationship. Interestingly, while the term "girlfriend" started to gain traction in the vernacular, it didn't immediately carry the weight it does today. Many women often stepped into romantic roles as "fiancés" or "sweethearts," while "girlfriend" was seen as a more casual term, lacking the serious commitment associated with traditional courtship. On the flip side, the word "boyfriend" showed up later in the narrative. This term gained popularity in the early 20th century, somewhere around the 1900s. Similar to "girlfriend," the term "boyfriend" is composed of "boy"—which historically referred to a young male, derived from the Old English "cniht" meaning "youth"— and "friend." Initially, "boyfriend" didn't imply a romantic relationship, either. Instead, it often encompassed a sense of camaraderie, friendships, and social interactions among young males.

As the century rolled on, the meaning of "boyfriend" became more synonymous with romantic involvement. By the mid-20th century, it was firmly established in

American slang to denote a serious romantic partner. It's worth noting that both of these terms had a significant surge in usage during the 1960s and 1970s, coinciding with a cultural shift—the sexual revolution.

What was the sexual revolution, you ask? The sexual revolution was heralded as a period of profound change in Western societies; it was the new age movement of that time. Many of the people in that era wanted to be liberated from what they considered to be the restrictive norms surrounding sexuality, so they stood against traditional roles and expectations. In short, they stood against the Word of God. This ushered in an era where sexual expression, personal freedom, and individual rights were championed, and the Word of God was all-the-more ignored or viewed as restrictive, constrictive, and outdated. However, the movement was a demonic shift, rather than a progressive one. Sure, the movement appeared to be grounded in a progressive delusion of equality and empowerment, the aftermath of this revolution invited in a lot of issues, strongholds, and demons that we still fight against today, including a greater percentage of divorces, far more single-parent households, a rise in crime, etc. Regardless of what the people wanted, the consequences and implications that have arisen from this seismic shift in sexual paradigms has nearly destroyed our country's moral fabric and weakened us as a nation. This is what spiritual warfare looks like. It's when the flesh takes center stage, pushing back against a norm that, quite frankly, has already been perverted. Remember, the devil thinks in generations. With each generation, he pushes against a norm, a tradition, or anything that keeps society following biblical principles, and he introduces what he disguises as freedom, independence, and what the world has come to know as autonomy. But before he can do this, he has to convince each generation that they are victims of the older generation's failures, thus highlighting the flaws, strongholds, and issues in each generation's predecessors. He then promotes what he disguises as a better way. Understand this—better is an enemy of good. Anything that God created, He called it good. Check out the following scriptures:

- **Genesis 1:3:** And God said, Let there be light: and there was light. And God saw the light, that it

<u>was good</u>: and God divided the light from the darkness.

- **Genesis 1:9-10:** And God said, Let the waters under the heaven be gathered together unto one place, and let the dry land appear: and it was so. And God called the dry land Earth; and the gathering together of the waters called he Seas: and <u>God saw that it was good</u>.

- **Genesis 1:12:** And the earth brought forth grass, and herb yielding seed after his kind, and the tree yielding fruit, whose seed was in itself, after his kind: and <u>God saw that it was good</u>.

- **Genesis 1:18-19:** And to rule over the day and over the night, and to divide the light from the darkness: and <u>God saw that it was good</u>. And the evening and the morning were the fourth day.

- **Genesis 1:21:** And God created great whales, and every living creature that moveth, which the waters brought forth abundantly, after their kind, and every winged fowl after his kind: and <u>God saw that it was good</u>.

- **Genesis 1:25:** And God made the beast of the earth after his kind, and cattle after their kind,

and every thing that creepeth upon the earth
after his kind: and <u>God saw that it was good</u>.

- **Genesis 1:31:** And God saw every thing that he
  had made, and, behold, <u>it was very good</u>.

The word "good" was used seven times in Genesis,
meaning good is good enough. However, in Genesis 3, a
sly little serpent walked into the Garden of Eden and
offered Eve something "better." In Genesis 2:16-17, we
find God giving Adam a set of instructions about his
restrictive diet; it reads, "And the LORD God commanded
the man, saying, Of every tree of the garden thou
mayest freely eat: But of the tree of the knowledge of
good and evil, thou shalt not eat of it: for in the day
that thou eatest thereof thou shalt surely die." Later on
in this chapter, we witness Eve being created, and in
Genesis 3, we find her encountering the serpent that
we'd all come to know as Satan. Genesis 3:1-5 reads,
"Now the serpent was more subtil than any beast of the
field which the LORD God had made. And he said unto the
woman, Yea, hath God said, Ye shall not eat of every tree
of the garden? And the woman said unto the serpent, We
may eat of the fruit of the trees of the garden: But of

the fruit of the tree which is in the midst of the garden, God hath said, Ye shall not eat of it, neither shall ye touch it, lest ye die. And the serpent said unto the woman, Ye shall not surely die: For God doth know that in the day ye eat thereof, then your eyes shall be opened, and ye shall be as gods, knowing good and evil." In this, Satan was promising Eve a better existence. Why would she have to rely on a God who restricted her when she can be as "gods" knowing good and evil. In other words, he introduced her to three concepts:

- Autonomy.
- Becoming her own god.
- Polytheism.

He said she would be as "gods," introducing her to the lie that there were other "gods" out there, thus suggesting that YAHWEH was one of many gods. All the same, he convinced her that YAHWEH was gate-keeping the truth from her, likely to keep her and her husband subject to Him. So, when Eve bit into the forbidden fruit, she wasn't just disobeying God, she was trying to become her own God, meaning she was, in a sense, filing for a divorce from God. What she, and many people who've come after her, did not realize was that the enemy of good is better. The wife God gives you is good enough. The husband God gives you is good enough. The children, pets, houses, cars, and revelation that God gives you is good enough. Understanding this truth opens the door for gratitude, and God loves a cheerful giver. However, when you shut the door in the face of gratitude, you simultaneously open up the door of victimhood. Satan had to convince Eve that she was a victim before he could get her to obey him, instead of obeying God. Again, he did this by lying to her and causing her to believe that God had been dishonest with her. And Satan still plays the same game with each generation. Every generation thinks they are smarter and more progressive than their predecessors, thus setting the stage for pride.

At its core, the sexual revolution sought to dismantle the traditional views of sexuality that had, for centuries, dictated the behavior and societal roles of individuals, particularly women. The advent of the birth control pill, the legal battles over abortion rights, and a burgeoning awareness of LGBTQ+ rights epitomized a dramatic reshaping of our moral and spiritual landscape.

One of the alarming outcomes of the sexual revolution is the pervasive normalization of casual sexual encounters or, better yet, the normalization of fornication and promiscuity. The rise of the "hook-up culture" has managed to redefine and reroute relationships, particularly among younger generations. What once was viewed as a deeply personal, sacred, and intimate act has often become a casual transaction between two or more souls. It is an orgy of sorts, and quite frankly, it is also a ritual. Understand this—when Eve bit into the forbidden fruit, she was practicing witchcraft in that moment. How so? Rebellion is as the sin of witchcraft (see 1 Samuel 15:23); we've read this time after time, but she was promised a spiritual result from performing a natural action. She would become her own god and know all things. All she had to do was eat the forbidden fruit. This was a ritual. The same is true for fornication. Satan promises the participants a desired result, oftentimes marriage, popularity, freedom from societal norms, a sense of empowerment, etc. He loves to make every generation feel emasculated, victimized, misunderstood, and controlled; this is how he sets the stage for revolutions, civil unrest, and civil wars.

The sexual revolution came about after an outcry against traditional courtships, where many of the youth wanted to have more casual relationships as opposed to intentional ones. Historically, courtship was a structured process; it was distinctly different from the modern conception of dating. In earlier societies, particularly during the 19th and early 20th centuries, courtship was often an informal engagement between potential partners, typically sanctioned by the families involved. Young people did not engage in casual dating; instead, their interactions were heavily influenced by cultural norms, economic considerations, and familial approvals. Courtship rituals were laden with social expectations, where the emphasis was on eloquence, propriety, and the demonstration of character. These rituals often served practical purposes, such as facilitating marital arrangements that aligned with social standings and material stability. In such a context, romance was an idealized component—at times, something to be considered rather than the primary motivation. In other words, traditionally, the focus was marriage, success, and following the rules and roles assigned by society. And of course, their way back then was closer to the arranged marriage construct found in the Bible. Marriage back then was less about looks and romance, and more about purpose, generational wealth, and building strong families, since strong families build strong communities.

However, societal transformations throughout the 20th century brought about a shift in how individuals approached romantic relationships. The latter part of the 1920s marked a significant turning point, coinciding with changes in gender roles, the advent of the automobile, and the influence of urbanization. Young individuals began to seek greater independence from cultural norms and traditions; this lead to the emergence of dating as a casual and exploratory pursuit, often detached from the traditional and biblical constraints of courtship. The dating revolution arose, characterized by a focus on personal choice and individual preferences, rather than familial or social obligations. And get this—individualism (or any ism, for that matter) precedes movements that pervert and ultimately destroy families, societies, and the world at large.

What a lot of women back then didn't realize was how important the presence and voice of a father was. You see, during this phase and stage, feminism began to take center-seat, and a lot of women began to rebel against the traditional roles assigned to women. And while this wasn't entirely bad, a lot of women took it too far. Fathers used to inspect the men who came after their daughters; this, of course, was after the courtship era and during the dating era. And just like in the biblical times, many fathers protected their daughters from wayward men who had no long term plans for themselves or a family—men who saw women as objects instead of human beings. But a lot of the fathers are at blame as well because many women suffered through abuse at the hands of their husbands, and their daughters witnessed this. They knew how society saw women; they knew that their mothers, in many cases, could not afford to leave their abusive, narcissistic, and oftentimes alcoholic husbands. This is because society frowned upon divorce. But understand that, once again, the devil thinks in generations. He knew that having a generation of broken and narcissistic men who abused their wives and children, and had multiple affairs would lead the next

generation to rebel against tradition. He would repeat
this cycle generation after generation, highlighting the
flaws from one generation to the next, creating discord
between generations. This way, the older generation
could not impart wisdom into the next generation
because the younger generation had witnessed their
fathers' nakedness. In other words, they'd seen their
fathers at their worst. And I am in no way promoting
that the old ways of doing things should have been
preserved. I am saying, however, that we have to divide
culture and tradition from God's Word, because when we
mix the two, religion is born, and religion often chases
people out of the church and away from God.

What was and is a concubine? Remember, when dealing
with the spiritual realm, you must think along the lines
of legalities. This will help you to better understand how
to address both soulish and spiritual matters.

In the biblical context, a concubine is typically defined
as a woman who is in a recognized, though subordinate,
marital relationship with a man, distinct from a fully
married wife. This relationship was characterized by its

social and legal legitimacy, albeit lacking some of the rights afforded to wives. The primary purpose of concubinage in these ancient societies was often associated with ensuring lineage, augmenting family size, and securing the transmission of property and status. A concubine, plainly put, was a woman who was legally bound to a man, but she held a lower status than his wife. She was considered a secondary wife; a sex toy of sorts, whose primary purpose was to bear children (especially male heirs) for her master and to appease him sexually.

The earliest references to concubines can be found in the Old Testament, where notable patriarchs, such as Abraham, Jacob, and David, had concubines alongside their wives. For instance, in the case of Abraham, we encounter Hagar, an Egyptian concubine who bore him a son by the name of Ishmael. Hagar's narrative is pivotal as it showcases the tensions and complexities arising from her status as a concubine, particularly in relation to Sarah, Abraham's primary wife. This situation highlights the dynamics that are inherent in polygamous relationships, marked by jealousy and conflict over issues of legitimacy and favoritism. Similarly, Jacob's relationships with Leah and Rachel exemplify the practice of concubinage. Rachel, unable to bear children, offered her maid, Bilhah, to Jacob as a concubine, thus utilizing the institution to fulfill cultural expectations regarding fertility and progeny.

In ancient Near Eastern societies, including those of the Canaanites, Mesopotamians, and Egyptians, concubinage was not only accepted but often socially demanded in elite circles as a means of political alliance, wealth accumulation, and social standing. The biblical text, while reflective of these cultural norms, also offers a unique moral lens on such practices, highlighting the inherent vulnerabilities and inequalities faced by concubines.

In layman's terms, a concubine was nothing but a glorified girlfriend. She was a woman set in place to be a sex slave, an incubator, and an ego booster for the man she served. She was an object of sorts, and while this wasn't frowned upon in those days, what most people don't know about concubines is that most of them were spoils of war, while others were gifts given to men by their own fathers. Then again, some concubines came about when their fathers failed to repay the debts they owed.

Spoils of War

One thing you've likely learned about the enemy is that he will attack his target until that target gives into his demands. He's been doing this in many of our families, generation after generation, destroying the men and perverting the women. After he'd managed to capture the minds of our ancestors, grandparents, and parents, we became the spoils of war. This is because we had to bear the weight of the generational curses they passed on to us. And we've had to sit on the sidelines and wonder why our families are so dysfunctional, not realizing that we are looking at bound people—we are looking at people who are chained to ungodly, downtrodden, and animalistic mindsets.

Gifts

Let's call a gift what it is—an offering. And offerings are often given to deities. For example, Sarai (later to be known as Sarah) gave her maiden, Hagar, to her husband, Abram (later to be known as Abraham), as a gift. Her goal and her role, at this point, was to bear a son for Abram, not realizing that God wasn't going to give Abram (the old man) a son. He was giving Abraham (the new man (a son). The old man would have implanted his old nature, but God wanted to do a new thing. Rachel and Leah would go on to repeat this same event, competing with one another for Jacob's love and affection. They gave their maidens to their shared husband so that he could get those women pregnant. Let it be known that a gift could and can only be given by its master or the person who owns the gift.

Consider the girlfriend/boyfriend pandemic today. Satan gives girlfriends and boyfriends as gifts or party favors to the people who are serving him, but YAHWEH gives us spouses. "House and riches are the inheritance of fathers: and a prudent wife is from the LORD" (Proverbs 19:14). Now, don't mistake what I'm saying. I truly understand that culture today demands that we label the people in our lives, and the boyfriend/ girlfriend classification is designed to communicate to others that the people in question are spoken for. So, while there is nothing inherently wrong with the titles themselves, the origin and spirit behind those titles cannot be ignored. In such relationships, it's all about casualness, freedom to rebel against God's Word, and the ability to walk away without any legal implications. In other words, people today want to test drive other people for three, five, and fifteen years, without having any legal ties to those people. They want a clean getaway and a clean break whenever they've grown bored with their partners.

Remember, traditionally speaking, a woman's father gives her away at her wedding. When you sleep with someone, you have married that person, albeit illegally. An illegal marriage is called fornication. Fornication is far more than the act of sex outside of marriage, it is the state that a man or woman's heart is stationed in. Notice the suffix "ion" at the end of fornication. What does that suffix mean? Encyclopedia Britannica defines "ion" this way:

1. a: act or process
   - validation
   - refrigeration
   - rebellion

   b: result of an act or process
   - regulation
   - rejection

2. state or condition
   - perfection

Check out the Greek and Hebrew translations of the word "fornication."

Fornication		
	Hebrew	**Greek**
Word	Taznuth	Porneia
Meaning	Harlotry, whoredom, unfaithfulness	Sexual immorality, fornication
Definition	harlotry, idolatry	fornication, whoredom; met: idolatry.
Source	Lexicon	Lexicon

Notice that the word "fornication" also means "idolatry." Consider the men and women who marched and protested against courtship, fought for their rights to "bodily autonomy" and stood against both traditional and biblical marriages. What do those moments mirror?

- **Exodus 31:1-6:** And when the people saw that Moses delayed to come down out of the mount, the people gathered themselves together unto Aaron, and said unto him, Up, make us gods, which shall go before us; for as for this Moses, the man that brought us up out of the land of Egypt, we wot not what is become of him. And Aaron said unto them, Break off the golden earrings, which are in the ears of your wives, of your sons, and of your daughters, and bring them unto me. And all the people brake off the golden earrings which were in their ears, and brought them unto Aaron. And he received them at their hand, and fashioned it with a graving tool, after he had made it a molten calf: and they said, These be thy gods, O Israel, which brought thee up out of the land of Egypt. And when Aaron saw it, he built an altar before it; and Aaron made proclamation, and said, To morrow is a feast to the Lord. And they rose up early on the morrow, and offered burnt offerings, and brought peace offerings; and the people sat down to eat and to drink, and rose up to play.

- **Exodus 16:1-7:** And the whole congregation of the children of Israel murmured against Moses and Aaron in the wilderness: And the children of Israel said unto them, Would to God we had died by the hand of the Lord in the land of Egypt, when we sat by the flesh pots, and when we did eat bread to the full; for ye have brought us forth into this wilderness, to kill this whole assembly with hunger. Then said the Lord unto Moses, Behold, I will rain bread from heaven for you; and the people shall go out and gather a certain rate every day, that I may prove them, whether they will walk in my law, or no. And it shall come to pass, that on the sixth day they shall prepare that which they bring in; and it shall be twice as much as they gather daily. And Moses and Aaron said unto all the children of Israel, At even, then ye shall know that the Lord hath brought you out from the land of Egypt: And in the morning, then

ye shall see the glory of the Lord; for that he
heareth your murmurings against the Lord: and
what are we, that ye murmur against us?

If you go throughout the Bible, you will find that it is
not uncommon for the uncrucified to throw tantrums
because they want something other than God. It is the
fallen nature of man to chase idols; yes, even edible
ones. But getting back to the topic at hand, the Bible
tells us in 1 Corinthians 6:13, " Meats for the belly, and
the belly for meats: but God shall destroy both it and
them. Now the body is not for fornication, but for the
Lord; and the Lord for the body." Ice was not made for
the microwave. If you microwave ice, you will change its
design and purpose. Cell phones were not made to be
microwaved. If you microwave a cell phone, you will
destroy the phone and the microwave. Lamps were not
made to be placed underwater. If you tried to place your
plugged-in lamp underwater, both you and the lamp will
likely expire. This is to say that whenever something is
used outside of its design, destruction is inevitable. The
same is true for the body. Many diseases and issues in
the body are the direct result of illegal sexual activity.

Many of the malfunctions and dysfunctions of the mind have everything to do with what we've done with our bodies. A lot of people are broke because they are broken. I'm sharing this to show you how the misuse of our bodies will ultimately cause our minds and bodies to break. When the body breaks, we call the event infirmity, but when the mind breaks, we call it insanity (a mental breakdown, an anxiety attack, mental illness, etc.). This is to say that you were not designed to be some man's girlfriend or boyfriend. These relationships are mostly illegal, and remember, the spirit realm operates in legalities. When you commit a crime, Satan has a legal right to arrest or, better yet, bind you, and God can sentence you to life in a relationship that He's repeatedly delivered you from. To sentence you to a thing is what we call "reprobation."

The Law Dictionary defines the word "reprobation" this way:

1. In ecclesiastical law. The interposition of objections or exceptions; as. to the competency of witnesses, to the due execution of instruments offered in evidence and the like.

Merriam Webster defines "reprobate" this way:

1. to condemn strongly as unworthy, unacceptable, or evil
2. to refuse to accept : reject
3. to foreordain to damnation

Romans 1:26-32 reads, "For this cause God gave them up unto vile affections: for even their women did change the natural use into that which is against nature: And likewise also the men, leaving the natural use of the woman, burned in their lust one toward another; men with men working that which is unseemly, and receiving in themselves that recompense of their error which was meet. And even as they did not like to retain God in their knowledge, God gave them over to a reprobate mind, to do those things which are not convenient; being filled with all unrighteousness, fornication, wickedness, covetousness, maliciousness; full of envy, murder, debate, deceit, malignity; whisperers, backbiters, haters of God, despiteful, proud, boasters, inventors of evil things, disobedient to parents, without understanding, covenant-breakers, without natural affection, implacable, unmerciful: Who knowing the judgment of

God, that they which commit such things are worthy of death, not only do the same, but have pleasure in them that do them."

Now, in the aforementioned text, we see God turning people over to reprobate minds, no longer protecting them from going after whatever illicit affections, desires, and perversions they had. Instead, he allowed their lusts to overtake them. No one knows how much mercy and grace God has extended to them until He takes it away!

Now, let's get to the meat and potatoes. We've already discussed that a girlfriend is a modern-day concubine, just as a boyfriend is a modern-day pimp and male prostitute. Back in the biblical days, it was not uncommon for kings to have many wives and concubines, but they'd only have one queen. Consider the story of Ahab. The Bible doesn't mention any of his wives or concubines outside of Jezebel, but the Bible does tell us that he had 70 sons. It does not, however, tell us how many daughters he had. There's no way one woman had 70 children! All the same, we do know that Jezebel had three children, and they were Athaliah, Jehoram, and

Ahaziah. Where did the other 67 children come from? More than likely, they came from the king's wives and concubines. What is the difference between a wife and a concubine? A man or king's wives typically came from households where the fathers had good, upstanding names in the community. The fathers were not in debt to anyone, and they'd given their daughters to the men in question in exchange for a bride price. Concubines, on the other hand, were oftentimes slaves; they were women who had been taken after a war had been won, a debt hadn't been paid, or in some instances, they were women who'd been summoned to audition for a queenship role, but they weren't chosen as the queen. Howbeit, after having spent the night with the king, they could not be sent home because the rule was—once a woman had been deflowered, it was dishonorable for the man who'd slept with her to return her to her father. This is because she would be considered "defiled" and it was improper for a non-virgin (outside of a widowed woman) to become a Jewish man's wife. For lack of a better term, such a woman was considered "damaged goods." It was the equivalent of returning a pair of worn underwear to a store and expecting them to restock the underwear for someone else to purchase. While it may sound cruel, this was the way they viewed unmarried women who were no longer virgins. Consider the story of King Xerxes, also known as King Aheuseurus, and Queen Esther. While the king was a pagan man who ran a pagan kingdom, many of the pagan nations copied and pasted Jewish culture, norms, and traditions. King Xerxes summoned all of the beautiful young virgins to his castle. He then chose the ones he liked the most to audition, sending the rest of the women home. The women who were chosen were prepared for one year, and after a year, they would all go and spend a night with the king. If the king favored them, he could potentially choose them as his next bride.

- **Esther 2:12-14:** Before a young woman's turn came to go in to King Xerxes, she had to complete twelve months of beauty treatments prescribed for the women, six months with oil of myrrh and six with perfumes and cosmetics. And this is how she would go to the king: Anything she wanted was given her to take with her from the harem to the king's palace. In the evening she would go there and in the morning return to another part of the harem to the care of Shaashgaz, the king's eunuch who was in charge of the concubines. She would not return to the king unless he was pleased with her and summoned her by name.

Get this—if a woman did not please the king, it was likely that she would never be summoned by him again. And while that doesn't sound too bad, the truth is—that woman would be considered the king's property, which meant that she could not go and be with another man— ever! So, if she hadn't gotten pregnant after their first encounter, she'd go the rest of her life childless. She would sit around and watch the king's favorite concubines be summoned time and time again, while her hope of ever being desired slowly withered away. It goes without saying that some of those women were probably happy that the king hadn't taken pleasure in them, but it was a high honor to bear children for a king, especially male heirs.

Let's step into today. Satan has convinced mankind to create a culture of concubinage, whereas, a bunch of "boyfriends" are now out on the loose looking for women that they can have a no-strings-attached relationship with, not realizing that in those relationships soul ties are still created, wounds are created, demons are transferred to and fro, and there some legalities present that, unbeknownst to the average person, does not allow the man to walk away scotch free. The same is true for women. When we illegally attach our souls to people, we allow people to step into places that are reserved for God and reserved for our Kingdom spouses. Consequently, we find ourselves falling time and time again into the trap of idolatry, thus summoning the Jezebel spirit (aka narcissist) to come into our lives. This happens when we follow the cultural norms that have been formed due to man's continuous revolutions and rebellions against the Most High. And it goes far deeper than this!

Once you enter fornication, you are placed or locked in the enemy's harem. No, this isn't a physical place; it's both mental and spiritual. This is when you'll notice that you:

1. Start to have a type.
2. Attract narcissistic people.
3. Relive the same experiences with different people.

What happens is, whatever devils that are in the person you slept with will now have access to you. This is what we call sexually transmitted demons. You see, demons can and do have appetites for people. This is the driving force behind obsession. Consider the story of Amnon and Tamar.

- **2 Samuel 13:1-19:** And it came to pass after this, that Absalom the son of David had a fair sister, whose name was Tamar; and Amnon the son of David loved her. And Amnon was so vexed, that he fell sick for his sister Tamar; for she was a virgin; and Amnon thought it hard for him to do anything to her. But Amnon had a friend, whose name was Jonadab, the son of Shimeah David's brother: and Jonadab was a very subtil man. And he said unto him, Why art thou, being the king's son, lean from day to day? wilt thou not tell me? And Amnon said unto him, I love Tamar, my brother Absalom's sister. And Jonadab said unto him, Lay thee down on thy bed, and make thyself sick: and when thy father cometh to see thee, say unto him, I pray thee, let my sister Tamar come, and give me meat, and dress the meat in my sight, that I may see it,

and eat it at her hand. So Amnon lay down, and
made himself sick: and when the king was come to
see him, Amnon said unto the king, I pray thee, let
Tamar my sister come, and make me a couple of
cakes in my sight, that I may eat at her hand. Then
David sent home to Tamar, saying, Go now to thy
brother Amnon's house, and dress him meat. So
Tamar went to her brother Amnon's house; and he
was laid down. And she took flour, and kneaded it,
and made cakes in his sight, and did bake the
cakes. And she took a pan, and poured them out
before him; but he refused to eat. And Amnon
said, Have out all men from me. And they went out
every man from him. And Amnon said unto Tamar,
Bring the meat into the chamber, that I may eat of
thine hand. And Tamar took the cakes which she
had made, and brought them into the chamber to
Amnon her brother. And when she had brought
them unto him to eat, he took hold of her, and said
unto her, Come lie with me, my sister. And she
answered him, Nay, my brother, do not force me;
for no such thing ought to be done in Israel: do
not thou this folly. And I, whither shall I cause my

shame to go? And as for thee, thou shalt be as one of the fools in Israel. Now therefore, I pray thee, speak unto the king; for he will not withhold me from thee. Howbeit he would not hearken unto her voice: but, being stronger than she, forced her, and lay with her. **Then Amnon hated her exceedingly**; so that the hatred wherewith he hated her was greater than the love wherewith he had loved her. And Amnon said unto her, Arise, be gone.

Wait! How did he go from loving her to hating her? Simply put, he lusted after her. And while the Bible doesn't mention this being a demonic infestation on Amnon's part, this is exactly what unclean spirits do! They love to infiltrate the imaginations of people and cause them to become obsessed with other people. Yes, even the idea of marrying and forming a family with certain people, but once their agendas have been accomplished, they'll stop giving those people beautiful imaginations of their love interests, and start harassing them with negative imaginations of those people. Again, this is why God told us to cast down imaginations and every high thing that exalts itself against the knowledge of God, and bring every thought captive to the obedience of Christ. You've likely experienced this; most people have. Someone pursued you with vigor, and at first, you resisted, but once you finally gave in, that person seemed to lose interest, especially if you sinned with them. Yes, it could have been a simple lust issue, but in many cases, it goes beyond the whelms and realms of human desire. In many cases, you are dealing with someone who needs deliverance, and their demons want access to you more than they do. Once access has been granted, they don't have to keep the two of you together to access you. Sin would have then given them a legal right to you, and again, they'll use the soul tie created in that illegal interaction/transaction to monitor, access, and attack you. This is because concubines belong to their kings as long as they live or as long as the king lives.

Satan knew what he was doing when he had those men and women out in the early to late 1900s wearing colorful clothes or, in many cases, naked, protesting for what they claimed to be their freedom. And in every generation, we will continue to see these movements that take society further and further away from God.

Our goal and assignment, as believers, is to have no fellowship with the unfruitful works of darkness, but rather reprove them (see Ephesians 5:11). If you've allowed yourself to be dated, humped, and dumped, you've signed up for a system and a stronghold. To break this, you have to:

1. Repent for fornication.
2. Return to God and do things His way.
3. Break up and break ties with any person who wants your body, but does not want to have matching last names with you.
4. Study the Word of God (consistently) to show yourself approved; in other words, take the Word and store it in your heart so you won't sin against God.
5. Go through deliverance and divorce the devil.
6. Avoid fornicators unless you're ministering to them.
7. Get therapy. Therapy is a great tool to aid you in your walk with Christ.
8. Take yourself off the dating market until you heal and until God gives you the clearance to go back out there, but in the meantime, follow Matthew

6:33, which reads, "But seek ye first the kingdom of God, and his righteousness; and all these things shall be added unto you."

9. Get rid of anything and everything that ties you to that person (except the kids and the pets). Remember that witches and warlocks use items like clothes, hair, gifts, etc. as points of contact; this allows them to better perform their rituals. Demons do the same. Those notes, teddy bears, and gifts that your exes gave you are all points of contact for the enemy, and he will use them to seduce, manipulate, or drag you back into the soul ties he's used to bind you.

Also, be sure to commit to a lifestyle of abstinence, reminding yourself that fornication isn't just an act; it is a state of mind, a condition, and a stronghold. You break its hold by coming out of idolatry. You come out of idolatry by repenting, being honest about where you are, and praying for wisdom, guidance, and instruction. You will succeed if you make up your mind to do so. Simply remind yourself daily, "I am somebody's wife or husband, and I am the daughter (or son) of the King of kings. Let me act accordingly."

LEVELS OF THE MIND

> Jesus said unto him, Thou shalt love the Lord thy God with
> all thy heart, and with all thy soul, and with all thy mind.
> Matthew 22:37

Did you know that, according to the world of psychology,
the mind can be broken down into three dimensions?
They are:

Conscious Mind   Subconscious Mind   Unconscious Mind

And before someone bellows out, "Show me this in the
Bible!" please note that there is a difference between
facts and truths, and facts are not necessarily enemies
of the truth unless they try to discredit the Word. The
Truth is the Word of God, and it is established in Heaven
as it is on Earth, but a fact is a lower-level truth that is
established only on Earth. A fact can be temporary, and
it can be disproved, but the Truth reigns true forever.
This is to say that, as the church, we don't necessarily
have to wage war with science, after all, true science
confirms God's Word, whereas, science that has been
mishandled tends to challenge the Word of God. Take a

look at the table below to get a better grasp of the
soul's makeup.

Conscious	Subconscious	Unconscious
30-Fold	60-Fold	100-Fold
Outer Court	Inner Court	Most Holy Place
Waiting Room	Heart	Operating Room

Let's start with the conscious. This is the waiting room
of the mind; this is where information goes to be tested
and considered before it is approved or rejected. For
example, the Bible tells us that when Eve looked at the
forbidden fruit, after having been tempted by the snake,
and that she "saw that the tree was good for food, and
that it was a delight to the eyes, and that the tree was
to be desired to make one wise." This simply means that
she took the devil's words into consideration. The way
this process looks is—she took an already established
truth that was in her heart and placed it back in the
outer courts of her mind. From there, she measured the
truth next to the lie, and she decided to believe the lie in
place of the truth, meaning she'd evicted the truth from
the garden of her mind and replaced that truth with a

lie. Consequently, she, along with her husband, was evicted from the Garden of Eden; this is because, once again, the spirit realm is like a huge mirror. We reap on this side what we sow on that side. Let's look at this a little deeper.

The conscious mind stores the information that it takes in, and that information partners with other information in its attempt to make its way into our hearts (belief systems). When it finds similar or like information in the head, we then experience what we call confirmation. We can keep information in our heads (conscious) for years, and even for a lifetime, never truly believing in that information, but we can keep hosting it as theories or information that we repeatedly or occasionally take into consideration. The information in the heart or, better yet, the subconscious mind, on the other hand, is information that we've labeled as truths or facts. This information has a magnetic pull to it. A better way of saying this is—let's say that you've come to believe that the Earth is flat. You've established this as a fact in your life, so it no longer sits in the waiting room or conscious realm of your mind. It's now integrated itself into your belief system; it is now in your heart. The heart, according to God's Word, is where the issues of life flow from. So, the information from the head flows to the heart, but the information and issues of the heart flow into our lives. And if you've come to believe that the Earth is flat, any information that seems to side with this theory would be information that you would speedily consider and invite into your heart as a fact. This is because it aligns with what you already believe. A better example would be this—a middle-aged man takes to the internet to tell anyone who will listen that all women are narcissistic, self-centered, egotistical creatures who hate men, love money, and only date men to get access to their money. He may very well believe this based on his experiences with his mother, the women in his family, and the women he's repeatedly chosen as romantic partners. So, while what he's proclaiming isn't true, it may be his truth, meaning it will repeatedly come to pass in his life because he believes it, he proclaims it, and he expects it. Any time that man comes across a video of a man being mishandled, abused, taken advantage of, or falsely accused by a woman, he will likely find himself having a heightened emotional response. In this, he may get angered and animated, so much so that he elects to go live and share the details of the story. If a false religion were to arise—one that is a branch or a false branch of Christianity—a branch that subjugates and abuses women, promoting the claim that women have to be controlled, abused, and kept on a tight leash, that man would likely join that religion. This has everything to do with the fact that in his heart or subconscious, he's come to believe that all women are inherently evil creatures. So, while many true believers may introduce him to the truth of God's Word, he may store that information in his conscious mind, not allowing it to enter his heart, however, the moment a bunch of false principles are presented to him, he'll give that information an all-access pass into his heart. Why? Because what's already in his heart will pull on that information; it aligns with what he's already come into agreement with. Get this—that's why we need to seek first the Kingdom of God and His righteousness, and according to Matthew 6:33, everything else will be added to us. When the truth is in your heart, it is attracted to the truth, and it will repel and reject any lie that enters your head. However, whenever lies occupy the subconscious or, better yet, the heart, those lies will repel the truth. This is why Jesus said in John 8:32, "And ye shall know the truth, and the truth shall make you free." This is also why the Word tells us in Hebrews 4:12, "For the word of God is quick, and powerful, and sharper than any two-edged sword, piercing even to the dividing asunder of soul and spirit, and of the joints and marrow, and is a discerner of the thoughts and intents of the heart." But in order for this to happen, you have to invite the truth in, test the spirit, taste and see that the Lord is good, and be willing to repent; that is, you have to be willing to turn away from the lies, renouncing and denouncing them, all the while turning to embrace the truth.

Read this carefully—the enemy will stop at nothing (but the Word) to fill your heart with lies. As a matter of fact, some of the strongest deliverance cases that I've come face-to-face with involved individuals who'd come to believe that God was mad at them, God had turned His back on them, and that they were hell bound. Deliverance sessions that could have and would have taken 15-30 minutes to complete can easily end up taking 6 or 7 hours simply because the person needing deliverance has embraced a false belief as it relates to God. And telling the demon to come out will prove to be ineffective until the person hosting that demon rejects those lies and allows the truth to enter their heart. This is why deliverance counseling is so important. This is also why therapy is important. In those cases, what set the stage for their freedom was (in most instances) God telling me to tell them that He's not mad at them, that He forgives them, or that He loves them. I've had cases where the demon has screamed out of people's mouths, "No, don't tell her that! Don't tell her that!" This is because the devil knew that those words were the key to that person's deliverance.

According to the world of psychology, we have on average 6,000-60,000 thoughts a day, 80% of which are negative, and 90% of which are repetitive. That's how much spiritual warfare we go through on any given day. Think about that! And because many of these thoughts are repetitive, we've likely grown accustomed to them. This means that we don't fight them anymore. We may not necessarily believe them, but they can get access to our hearts if they find other thought bubbles to unite themselves to. Again, this can set the stage for confirmation, and confirmation leads to conformation. This is to say that the lies in your heart have to be challenged because they are producing the issues that you've found flowing in and out of your life. All the same, you have to learn to masterfully guard your heart with the Word of Truth, resisting the temptation to connect with any person who loves the world and what it has to offer.

Last, but not least, there is the unconscious mind. This is where we store memories, habits, desires, traumas, and some of our most ingrained beliefs. This is also where our emotions are housed, and believe it or not, demons can and do get access to people's emotions. Unclean spirits cannot get access to any sector of a believer's unconscious mind, but they can affect and infect the information that goes into it. All the same, it is difficult for them to access this space in an unbeliever's mind, but whenever they do, that unbeliever will experience a full-on demonic possession. This is the sector of the mind that controls breathing and how we react to stimuli. This is what the Bible refers to as the "spirit of the mind." If demons get access to this portion of a person's mind, that person has been turned over to a reprobate mind.

Think of your mind as a garden; it is your own personal Garden of Eden. In this garden, you will either plant truths or you will allow the enemy to plant lies. If you plant and water the truth, you will see the fruits of the Spirit begin to grow in your life. They are:

Love	Joy	Peace
Patience	Kindness	Goodness
Faithfulness	Gentleness	Self Control

People often ask the million-dollar question, and that is, "How do you test the spirit of a person?" It's simple. The Bible says that you will know them by their fruit. What fruits, you ask? The fruits of the Spirit or the works of the flesh. But, please keep in mind that the Word is one. While you see a lot of books, chapters, paragraphs, and words in the Bible, the Word is a single unit. This is to say that the whole Bible is a system; it is interconnected. With that said, the Bible says in Matthew 7:3-5, "And why beholdest thou the mote that is in thy brother's eye, but considerest not the beam that is in thine own eye? Or how wilt thou say to thy brother, Let me pull out the mote out of thine eye; and, behold, a beam is in thine own eye? Thou hypocrite, first cast out the beam out of thine own eye; and then shalt thou see clearly to cast out the mote out of thy brother's eye."

- What destroys trust? Hypocrisy!
- What destroys relationships? Hypocrisy!
- What destroys covenants? You guessed it—hypocrisy!

In this, God is telling us to not do a fruit inspection in someone else's life if we have not inspected our own fruits. Our assignment is to pursue God so that we can grow the fruits of the Spirit in our lives, and we can change the nature and soil of our gardens by eradicating the works of the flesh. This is how discernment breaks through our soil! Most people date and soul-tie themselves to demonically led people, not because they themselves are inherently bad people, but because they didn't grow the fruits of the Spirit in their lives enough to pluck out the weeds that grow in their gardens. These weeds are what the Bible refers to as the works of the flesh; they are:

Adultery	Fornication	Uncleanness
Lasciviousness	Idolatry	Witchcraft
Hatred	Variance	Emulations
Wrath	Strife	Seditions
Heresies	Envyings	Murders
Drunkenness		Revelings

These are the many works of the flesh that the Bible warns against. All the same, your goal is to avoid forming romantic and platonic relationships with people who bear these fruits. Now, don't get me wrong—in order to evangelize and win the souls of the lost, we have to form relationships with them. However, the type of relationship you form will determine the strength of the soul tie that is established between you and that person, and how that soul tie is used. This is why Apostle Paul said in 1 Corinthians 15:33, "Be not

deceived: evil communications corrupt good manners."
Apostle Paul also went on to say, in 1 Corinthians 5:11,
"But now I have written unto you not to keep company,
if any man that is called a brother be a fornicator, or
covetous, or an idolator, or a railer, or a drunkard, or an
extortioner; with such an one no not to eat." The reason
for these instructions is because an unbeliever, a
backsliding believer, a lukewarm believer, and a double-
minded believer can easily poison your perspective and
turn your heart away from God or, at minimum, the soul
tie you have with that person could become a bridge that
their demons use to visit and harass you. It can also be
used as a lasso, whereas demons will drag, stretch, pull,
and repeatedly put a strain on your relationships in an
attempt to control and dominate you. So, you may find
that you haven't thought about the opposite sex in four
years. You've remained abstinent, and you've been
focusing your attention on God and doing what He's
instructed you to do, but after meeting a new friend
(we'll call her Charlotte), you are now wrestling with
lust issues. The issue here could be that Charlotte
wrestles with, and may even submit herself to, the
spirits of lust and lasciviousness. This is to say that

your soul tie with Charlotte is now being use to pervert, seduce, and mislead you. This is why so many true men and women of God have fallen repeatedly into sexual sin, as well as other sins. This is also why many of them have fallen away from God. They, with good intentions, connected themselves in the wrong way to the wrong people without praying first. God will tell you who to connect to and how to connect to those people. He will also tell you who not to connect to, and how to avoid those connections. This means that we have to be proactive when it comes to prayer, rather than making what seems to be a good decision first, and then reacting later once we find ourselves in yet another satanic snare.

Satan can use people in our lives to drag us away from God's will, drag us out of God's presence, and seduce us into the darkness with promises of favor, pleasure, and blessings. But he can do this most effectively when we've formed soul ties with those people, and they've grown to become valuable and even invaluable fixtures in our lives. However, he can't successfully form those soul ties unless he convinces us to stop guarding our hearts;

this way, he can implant lies into our hearts.

Whatever we feed our souls is our soul's food, whether we are repeatedly eating the fruits of the Spirit or feasting on the works of the flesh. This will determine what we crave day after day. So, if you are always giving into the temptation to fornicate, masturbate, and indulge in sexual sin, you will continue to crave illegal sex. However, if you are continuously studying the Word of God, you will find that your soul will, over time, begin to crave the Word. Whatever you store in your heart will be the very thing that you will repeatedly seek. This will determine the soul ties that you repeatedly form with people, your ability to cleave, and the issues that flow from your life. So, plant the garden you want to eat from, and uproot the weeds that come to choke out what is good and Godly in your life.

Soul Binders

> For the word of God is quick, and powerful, and sharper than any two-edged sword, piercing even to the dividing asunder of soul and spirit, and of the joints and marrow, and is a discerner of the thoughts and intents of the heart.
> Hebrew 4:12

A soul tie is a soul's tie; in simplistic terms, it means that a person's soul is tied to the soul of another individual, but to be "soul tied to" and "soul tied by" are two different scenarios. We are soul tied to people, but we are tied to those people by one of many issues. In this chapter, we will explore the binders that are commonly used to bind our souls to other people. This way, we can effectively sever any and all ungodly soul ties that are holding us captive.

Did you know that soul ties were often used as weapons of warfare? Consider the story of Saul and David. Saul's jealousy of David became an extension of his madness. And in his crazed state, he decided to use his daughter,

Merab, in marriage in an attempt to ensnare him, however, over time, Saul decided to marry Merab off to someone else. But he later learned that his daughter, Michal, had a crush on David, and he decided to use this to his advantage. Let's look at how this story played out.

- **1 Samuel 18:17-21:** And Saul said to David, Behold my elder daughter Merab, her will I give thee to wife: only be thou valiant for me, and fight the LORD's battles. For Saul said, Let not mine hand be upon him, but let the hand of the Philistines be upon him. And David said unto Saul, Who am I? And what is my life, or my father's family in Israel, that I should be son in law to the king? But it came to pass at the time when Merab Saul's daughter should have been given to David, that she was given unto Adriel the Meholathite to wife. And Michal Saul's daughter loved David: and they told Saul, and the thing pleased him. And Saul said, I will give him her, that she may be a snare to him, and that the hand of the Philistines may be against him. Wherefore Saul said to David, Thou shalt this day be my son in law in the one of the twain.

- **2 Samuel 6:16:** And as the ark of the Lord came into the city of David, Michal Saul's daughter looked through a window, and saw king David leaping and dancing before the Lord; and she despised him in her heart.

- **2 Samuel 6:20-23:** Then David returned to bless his household. And Michal the daughter of Saul came out to meet David, and said, How glorious was the king of Israel to day, who uncovered himself to day in the eyes of the handmaids of his servants, as one of the vain fellows shamelessly uncovereth himself! And David said unto Michal, It was before the LORD, which chose me before thy father, and before all his house, to appoint me ruler over the people of the LORD, over Israel: therefore will I play before the LORD. And I will yet be more vile than thus, and will be base in mine own sight: and of the maidservants which thou hast spoken of, of them shall I be had in honour. Therefore Michal the daughter of Saul had no child unto the day of her death.

The daughters of kings were often given away in marriage by their fathers to men of power, so David was right to question Saul's reasoning. Our brains are trained to see the moment when David asked himself, "Who am I, and what is my life, or my father's family in Israel, that I should be the son-in-law of the king?" as humility on his part when, in truth, this was a moment of discernment. Howbeit, like most of us, David likely filled in the blanks and told himself that he was overthinking everything. What David didn't know was that his fight against Goliath had put him, a mere shepherd boy, on the Philistine's radar. Ordinarily, they wouldn't know too much about or even target a soldier, and they likely viewed David's victory over Goliath as a mere stroke of luck. However, it goes without saying that they were monitoring the inner-workings of the Israelites, waiting for the perfect moment to attack them. So, hearing that the guy who'd killed and decapitated one of their mightiest warriors was gearing up to marry the king's daughter would undoubtedly cause them to begin to plot and scheme against what could potentially be the future king of Israel. In other words, David's growing influence could have been seen as a threat to the Philistines and their government, and it was likely seen as a strategic move since David had been the one to kill Goliath. Saul believed that this move would be seen as a political one, which would potentially provoke the Philistines to assassinate David. This would keep his hands clean and his reputation clear amongst the Israelites. It would have and could have been the perfect plan, but there was one thing in the way of it all. The same God who'd protected David from Goliath and empowered him to kill Goliath was still with David. And amazingly enough, while Michal was totally unaware of her father's plans against David initially, she ultimately did become a weapon fashioned against him. After all, a father knows what he's instilled in his daughter. It's like fashioning a bomb with a timer attached, and then feeding it to a kitten, and then depriving that kitten of love and affection before releasing it into the arms of an animal lover. Once the kitten experiences love for the first time, it will likely become incredibly clingy, wanting to be in its master's arms or, at minimum, within a few feet of its master at all times, totally oblivious to the dangers within. This is what spiritual warfare looks like. The devil doesn't always deploy malicious people who, in secret, plot the downfall of God's people. Satan's favorite weapon is a person who doesn't know what

they're carrying, either good or bad. This is a lesson
many leaders have had to learn the hard way. People rush
towards leadership with their hearts wide open, eager to
soul tie themselves to these shepherds, and while many
have good intentions, they have bad hearts. Our good
intentions often come from the commercials that we
repeatedly play in our minds, but we don't think about
the bad times, the hard times, or the confusing times
that every relationship is tested by. We don't think
about the trials by fire, the seasonal shifts, or how we'll
respond when we're both being stretched. So, people can
and do soul tie themselves to leaders with good
intentions, but as always, life happens, and all too
often, the size of our pain ends up matching the size of
our expectations. Pain is pressure; it doesn't just feel
bad, it presses against the heart until what's in the
heart has no choice but to surface. I remember telling a
pastor friend of mine that I saw some people like hand
grenades that the enemy tosses into churches. The
people have good intentions. They don't have any evil
plans towards their pastors or their church family, but
they do have something in them that makes them more
dangerous than Jezebel herself, and that is an idolatrous

heart. Coupled with unrealistic expectations, an idolatrous heart causes people to crown their leaders as their lords and saviors, all the while acknowledging Jesus Christ as the Messiah. This infection of the soul leads them to fantasize about getting close to their leaders, hanging out with their leaders, traveling with their leaders, and just becoming a part of the leaders' entourage. They think that if this were to happen, they'd finally have the families they've always wanted, and this would cure them of anxiety, distrust, and trauma. This type of thinking is a symptom of rejection, idolatry, and (covert) control, which all point to the spirit of Jezebel. But again, the people in question have good intentions; they are totally unaware of what lies within their souls waiting to ambush anyone who gets close to him, especially leaders in the Lord's church. And most leaders put up loving but firm boundaries, which in turn, causes the spirit of rejection to rise in these unhealed souls. So, many people leave the churches that God placed them in, or they leave the traditional church scene altogether, believing that they've been wronged, misunderstood, or maybe even the victims of lies told by other congregants when, in truth, they had unrealistic expectations that were not met. If the leaders do allow them to get close, Satan's strategy is to then torment the people in question by causing them to hyper-fixate on their leaders' flaws, quirks, issues, choices, habits, and in some cases, the leaders' material possessions. On the church scene, this is called familiarity. And once the relationship enters this phase, the bombs start counting down until the torment causes the sheep to bite their shepherds or, at minimum, to suddenly break their commitments and walk away. In many cases, the people walk away and begin a verbal and virtual slander campaign against their leaders. Again, this is one of the strategies of spiritual warfare—Satan knows that if you have a heart of rejection and an idolatrous heart, you'd chase after people, wanting desperately to connect with them, prove yourself to them, and be an intricate part of their lives. He also knows how you handle negative stimuli, and how much pressure it takes to make what's in you explode. So, he'll try to get you to bind yourself to someone he wants to destroy, or he'll try to get someone to connect themselves to you so that what's in them could destroy you. And in some instances, he sends two people on a suicide mission, whereas, one person will destroy himself, destroy his ministry, and destroy his good reputation trying to destroy another soul.

Another example of a soul tie being used to ensnare a soul is in the oh-so-infamous story of Samson and Delilah. You can read the story in Judges 16, but did you know that Delilah, which by the way means "delicate" or "one who weakened" wasn't the only woman used to manipulate Samson? A group of men used Samson's first wife as a tool to win a bet against Samson prior to Delilah's arrival on the scene. You can find this story in Judges 14. In summary, Samson gave the guys a riddle. Let's look at the story in part. Judges 14:10-17 reads, "So his father went down unto the woman: and Samson made there a feast; for so used the young men to do. And it came to pass, when they saw him, that they brought thirty companions to be with him. And Samson said unto them, I will now put forth a riddle unto you: if ye can certainly declare it me within the seven days of the feast, and find it out, then I will give you thirty sheets and thirty change of garments: But if ye cannot declare it me, then shall ye give me thirty sheets and thirty change of garments. And they said unto him, Put forth thy riddle, that we may hear it. And he said unto them, Out of the eater came forth meat, and out of the strong came forth sweetness. And they could not in three days expound the riddle. And it came to pass on the seventh day, that they said unto Samson's wife, Entice thy husband, that he may declare unto us the riddle, lest we burn thee and thy father's house with fire: have ye called us to take that we have? is it not so? And Samson's wife wept before him, and said, Thou dost but hate me, and lovest me not: thou hast put forth a riddle unto the children of my people, and hast not told it me. And he said unto her, Behold, I have not told it my father nor my mother, and shall I tell it thee? And she wept before him the seven days, while their feast lasted: and it came to pass on the seventh day, that he told her, because she lay sore upon him: and she told the riddle to the children of her people." Of course, the woman told the riddle to the companions, they solved the riddle, Samson was upset, and his would-be father-in-law ended up giving Samson's wife to another man. This soul tie, unbeknownst to Samson and his parents, had been orchestrated by the Lord as a means of warfare against the Philistines (see Judges 14:4). This event set a war in

motion that would ultimately lead to a mass
slaughtering of the Philistines. Judges 15:1-8 shows us
how this event would ultimately put Samson on the
Philistines' radar; it reads, "But it came to pass within a
while after, in the time of wheat harvest, that Samson
visited his wife with a kid; and he said, I will go in to my
wife into the chamber. But her father would not suffer
him to go in. And her father said, I verily thought that
thou hadst utterly hated her; therefore I gave her to thy
companion: is not her younger sister fairer than she?
Take her, I pray thee, instead of her. And Samson said
concerning them, Now shall I be more blameless than the
Philistines, though I do them a displeasure. And Samson
went and caught three hundred foxes, and took
firebrands, and turned tail to tail, and put a firebrand in
the midst between two tails. And when he had set the
brands on fire, he let them go into the standing corn of
the Philistines, and burnt up both the shocks, and also
the standing corn, with the vineyards and olives. Then
the Philistines said, Who hath done this? And they
answered, Samson, the son in law of the Timnite,
because he had taken his wife, and given her to his
companion. And the Philistines came up, and burnt her

and her father with fire. And Samson said unto them, Though ye have done this, yet will I be avenged of you, and after that I will cease. And he smote them hip and thigh with a great slaughter: and he went down and dwelt in the top of the rock Etam." It was at this moment, the Philistines realized how powerful Samson was, and they sought to take his life, so they did what any skilled enemy would do. They monitored him, looking for an open door or an opportunity to ensnare him, and it did not take them long to discover Samson's stronghold—his lust for exotic women. You see, immediately after the slaughter, Samson went to Gaza, saw a prostitute, and then went and slept with her. Not long after this, he met Delilah, and she would be his undoing. The Philistines offered Delilah eleven hundred shekels of silver (5,500 pieces of silver each); this is the modern day equivalent of 1,100 pieces each from five of their lords. Today, this is estimated to be around $15 million. Yes, this is how badly they wanted to capture Samson! All the same, Delilah's method of attack mirrored that of Samson's first wife—she nagged him to death—literally. Please note that nagging is the natural equivalent of torment (mental torture). What is torment? It is repetition. According to Oxford Languages, it is "severe physical or mental suffering." The suffix "ing" implies a process, meaning it's not a quick kill. It is a process of torturing a soul until the person complies with the demands of the person or the power that's tormenting them. For example, waterboarding is a form of torture. According to Encyclopedia Britannica, waterboarding is defined a:

> "method of torture in which water is poured into the nose and mouth of a victim who lies on his back on an inclined platform, with his feet above his head. As the victim's sinus cavities and mouth fill with water, his gag reflex causes him to expel air from his lungs, leaving him unable to exhale and unable to inhale without aspirating water. Although water usually enters the lungs, it does not immediately fill them, owing to their elevated position with respect to the head and neck. In this way the victim can be made to drown for short periods without suffering asphyxiation. The victim's mouth and nose are often covered with a cloth, which allows water to enter but prevents it from being expelled; alternatively, his mouth may

be covered with cellophane or held shut for this purpose. The torture is eventually halted and the victim put in an upright position to allow him to cough and vomit (water usually enters the esophagus and stomach) or to revive him if he has become unconscious, after which the torture may be resumed. Waterboarding produces extreme physical suffering and an uncontrollable feeling of panic and terror, usually within seconds" (Source: Encyclopedia Britannica/water boarding/Brian Duignan).

This is torment; again, it's a form of torture. We call it torture when it's external pain, but we often refer to it as torment when it's a form of internal or mental pain. This is simply to point out that nagging is oftentimes a form of witchcraft. This is also to point out the fact that one of Satan's favorite brands of spiritual warfare and entertainment is to pair a man up with a woman who nags him, or to pair a woman up to a man who is inconsistent or unreliable; this way, they can bring the warfare from within the head (30-fold) to the house (60-fold), and ultimately to the heart (100-fold). Remember, the issues of life pour from the heart, but they start in the head.

- **Proverbs 27:15-16 (ESV):** A continual dripping on a rainy day and a quarrelsome wife are alike; to restrain her is to restrain the wind or to grasp oil in one's right hand.
- **Proverbs 21:9:** It is better to dwell in a corner of the housetop, than with a brawling woman in a wide house.
- **Proverbs 21:19:** It is better to dwell in the wilderness, than with a contentious and an angry woman.
- **Proverbs 25:19:** Confidence in an unfaithful man in time of trouble is like a broken tooth, and a foot out of joint.
- **Matthew 15:14:** Let them alone: they be blind leaders of the blind. And if the blind lead the blind, both shall fall into the ditch.

Another fact worth mentioning is that a human being can be soul tied to stuff, but material things have no soul, therefore, the soul tie would be one-sided. We see this evidenced in the story of the rich young ruler. Matthew 19:16-22 details this story. It reads, "And, behold, one came and said unto him, Good Master, what good thing shall I do, that I may have eternal life? And he said unto him, Why callest thou me good? There is none good but one, that is, God: but if thou wilt enter into life, keep the commandments. He saith unto him, Which? Jesus said, Thou shalt do no murder, Thou shalt not commit adultery, Thou shalt not steal, Thou shalt not bear false witness, honor thy father and thy mother: and, thou shalt love thy neighbor as thyself. The young man saith unto him, All these things have I kept from my youth up: what lack I yet? Jesus said unto him, If thou wilt be perfect, go and sell that thou hast, and give to the poor, and thou shalt have treasure in heaven: and come and follow me. But when the young man heard that saying, he went away sorrowful: for he had great possessions." Get this—the problem wasn't the fact that the guy was rich; this is important because people who aggressively believe but passively imply that Christians should have just enough or live beneath the poverty line often use this scripture to bash other Christians who are wealthy, driven, or business-minded. The issue in the aforementioned text was the fact that the rich guy relied on the very system and laws that Jesus had come to fulfill. This is why Jesus quoted the

Ten Commandments to him. Jesus knew that the Mosaic Law could not save anyone, so what was happening in this instance was the man was in the middle of a Messiah moment, meaning he was at the crossroads that served as an intersection between works (performance-based faith) and grace. But the guy was rich, and while the Bible doesn't tell us this, it is likely that his riches came from the very system that Jesus was telling him to forsake. After all, Jesus didn't just tell him to sell everything he owned, Jesus told him to come and follow Him. So, yes, the guy was soul-tied to his wealth, but he was also financially tied to the very system that was enriching him, while ensnaring his soul. The man wanted to know what he could "do" to have eternal life, but Jesus told him who he could "become" instead. Instead of having a private conversation in the backwoods of Judea, Jesus invited him into a public relationship with the Lord. Believe it or not, this relationship is called "ministry," and this is what a lot of believers run from today. They want private relationships with the Lord, but public relationships with the world. This is why Jesus said in Mark 8:38, "Whosoever therefore shall be ashamed of me and of my words in this adulterous and sinful generation; of him also shall the Son of man be ashamed, when he cometh in the glory of his Father with the holy angels."

And just like a soul tie can be used as a snare, God can and does use soul ties as a tool of salvation. Consider the story of Joseph. While he was locked away in prison, he met two people who would be pivotal to his deliverance and rise to power. He met Pharaoh's cup bearer and his baker. You can read this story in Genesis 40. In short, both the cup bearer and the baker had been imprisoned, and in prison is where they'd met Joseph. Both men had a dream in which they told to Joseph, and he interpreted their dreams for them. Genesis 40:9-18 (NIV) reads, "So the chief cupbearer told Joseph his dream. He said to him, 'In my dream I saw a vine in front of me, and on the vine were three branches. As soon as it budded, it blossomed, and its clusters ripened into grapes. Pharaoh's cup was in my hand, and I took the grapes, squeezed them into Pharaoh's cup and put the cup in his hand.'

'This is what it means,' Joseph said to him. 'The three branches are three days. Within three days Pharaoh will lift up your head and restore you to your position, and you will put Pharaoh's cup in his hand, just as you used to do when you were his cupbearer. But when all goes well with you, remember me and show me kindness; mention me to Pharaoh and get me out of this prison. I was forcibly carried off from the land of the Hebrews, and even here I have done nothing to deserve being put in a dungeon.'

When the chief baker saw that Joseph had given a favorable interpretation, he said to Joseph, 'I too had a dream: On my head were three baskets of bread. In the top basket were all kinds of baked goods for Pharaoh, but the birds were eating them out of the basket on my head.' 'This is what it means,' Joseph said. 'The three baskets are three days. Within three days Pharaoh will lift off your head and impale your body on a pole. And the birds will eat away your flesh.'" And just as Joseph had prophesied, these things did come to pass. However, the cup bearer forgot about Joseph for two years; that was until Pharaoh started having a series of dreams that none of his wise men or magicians could interpret. That's when the cup bearer remembered Joseph, told him about the young prophet, and the rest is history. Pharaoh summoned Joseph, and Joseph (through the Spirit of

God) successfully interpreted Pharaoh's dream, in addition to giving him wisdom. What happened next would change the trajectory of Joseph's life, and it would charter in a move of God that would challenge religion altogether. Like He'd done with Daniel and Esther in times' past, God would place Joseph in a pagan palace under a pagan ruler, but not for the rulers' sake. God did this to bless and protect His people. Joseph would go on to become Pharaoh's right-hand man; he would become his second in charge, also known as a Vizier.

As we can see, there are good and Godly soul ties; then again, there are ungodly and demonic soul ties, both of which are used to influence the choices of God's people. Now, let's talk binders! Every binding agent (worker) needs a binding agent (binder). According to Oxford Languages, a binder is "a **substance** used to make other **substances** or materials stick or mix together." What is faith? According to Hebrews 11:1, "Now faith is the **substance** of things hoped for, the evidence of things not seen." Notice it said "now faith," not "now, faith." This is because faith is never later; it is always now. Faith for later is called hope, and hope deferred or

delayed makes the heart sick (see Proverbs 13:12).
Below, is a table of binders that are used to form soul
ties. Note: this list, albeit exhaustive, is not a complete
list of binders, since just about anything that we want,
value, or fear can be used to bind our souls to the soul of
another person, place, event, time, or object.

Types of Binders	
Unforgiveness	Unforgiveness is debt placed on another individual, whether you feel like that person owes you a new car, couch, or an apology, refusing to move forward and release that person from his or her debt to you is unforgiveness. And it binds your soul to the individual in question. The evidence of this is the fact that the person would remain on your mind and in your heart until you forgave them, and whenever or if ever he or she suffers harm, you would likely rejoice; whenever or if ever the individual is blessed, you would be provoked.
Hatred	Like unforgiveness, hatred is having

	Satan's heart towards a person, and it can cause you to monitor the individual or invest too much of your time, thoughts, and resources into discussing or trying to hurt, harm, or sabotage the individual in question. This is what would serve to bind your soul to the individual. You'd still have that person on your mind. Consequently, their choices would still affect your feelings, thoughts, and choices.
Fear	Fear can tie you to a person, place, or thing; it can tie you to an event or a space in time. This is because fear is a form of reverence, and in order for you to fear something or someone, you have to establish in your heart that the person or whatever it is that you fear poses a credible threat to you. Fear is stored in the heart. Again, biblically speaking, this is the mind. This is why demons love to use the mechanism of fear to cross over from one person to the other, and they love

	to use fear to tie people together.
Love	God is Love, and Love is God, and He ties us all together in Him. So, whenever someone says that they love you, they are saying they have God's heart for you. If they don't have God's heart, it is impossible for them to have God's heart for you. In other words, if they aren't saved, they don't love you, they are feeling a different set of emotions that they think is love. Howbeit, true love binds two people together. All the same, love is not an emotion, contrary to popular belief. It is a fruit of the Spirit. There is an emotional aspect of love, but most of what's promoted today as love is lust and obsession in disguise.
Financial	A financial binder is called dependency and/or co-dependency. Some people are bound to the United States government because they perpetually rely on the government, some people are bound to certain members of their families,

	while others are financially tied to their lovers. Today, this is one of the most common soul ties, with many young adults too afraid to leave their parents' homes, electing to look for romantic partners that they can financially bind themselves to.
Familial	Familial soul ties are normal, but they can become toxic and demonic. A great example of a familial bind or bond can be found in large families, where members of these units regularly come together to eat, solidify their bonds, and discuss family matters. This sounds great until you've been a part of or been invited to one of these functions. In these gatherings, sin is promoted, demonic traditions are upheld, and stragglers are humbled and humiliated. Anyone who has broken away from the family and gone on to find Jesus, success, and healing is persecuted and used as an example of what not to do should you "get money." Of course, familial bonds can be found

	in our nuclear families as well, whereas you may find the narcissistic family unit, also known as the Dysfunctional Family Unit, and every person has been tamed, trained, and broken to perform in a certain role, often revering the narcissist (Jezebel) as the head of that unit.
Trauma	I'm sure we've all heard of trauma bonding. What is a trauma bond? Psychology Today reports the following: "A trauma bond in a relationship involves a foundation of abuse, which may hinge on tactics such as threats of harm, manipulation, control, shaming, gaslighting, and sabotage, mixed with intermittent moments of calm and displays of affection. This pattern of highs and lows increases a victim's unhealthy attachment to the abuser, which helps maintain the relationship." (Psychology Today/Trauma Bonding). People also establish trauma bonds by opening up and sharing their traumatic stories

	with other people. This increases the chances of them binding or soul-tying themselves to the people they're interested in or targeting, as most people let down their guards and open their hearts when people become vulnerable in front of them.
Emotional	Emotional soul ties are formed when people love-bomb, flatter, and open their hearts to other people. They can also form when someone displays a heightened negative emotion. I like to use the example of two women being in the workplace, with one of those women being jealous of the other woman. We will call the cruel and jealous woman Terri, and we'll call the other woman Melissa. Terri goes out of her way to give Melissa a hard time, often raising her voice at her, refusing to greet her, reporting her anytime she makes a mistake, and speaking reproachfully about her to a few of the women at the office. It goes without saying that Terri has made Melissa's

time at the office a living hell. But one day, Terri seems to have a change of heart. "Here," she says, handing Melissa a brown paper bag. "I brought you something to eat because I was concerned about you. Are you feeling okay? I noticed that you weren't your normal self today." Melissa is surprised, but she welcomes this moment. The two ladies talk, and after this, they become inseparable. This is a common wile or tactic of the enemy. More than likely, Terri envies Melissa and feels threatened by her presence, so she elected to make her tenure at the office difficult before offering her an olive branch in the form of a sandwich. You see, people like Terri like to keep their friends close but their enemies closer, so they like to create emotional bonds with their victims. Often displaying their negative emotions first; this way, their targets can become accustomed to their negative views of life, emotional

	outbursts, and their criticisms. This is a mechanism of control, and it is a form of emotional witchcraft. And again, some people will get you to open up by displaying their positive emotions, flattering you, and always trying to give you heightened emotional experiences. This allows them to bond with you emotionally, and you will notice that in those relationships, when things are great, they are AMAZING, but when things are bad, they are BEYOND TRAUMATIC.
Platonic	We form platonic soul ties with our friends, but get this, we can form platonic soul ties with our parents, our children, our lovers, our pastors, or anyone we invite into this space. Sometimes, this can be bad; other times, it can be demonic, especially in relationships that require a measure of trust and submission. For example, you can laugh and play with your children, after all, most parents do this, but at times, you may have to remind them

	that playing and joking around with them doesn't diminish your role as their parent. In this, you have to teach them how to have respect and honor, even in those moments when the authority figures in their lives are willing to let their hair down and just have fun.
Material	Similar to financial soul ties, you can bind yourself to stuff, just like material items can be used to establish a bond between you and another person. Most women have experienced a man giving them gifts, and then feeling as if those gifts entitled them (the men) to their bodies. This is why the older generation of women used to warn us with these words, "Don't take gifts from a man you don't see a future with." Another lesson I learned is—you can spoil grown folks. I'm a giver by nature; it's a part of my design and it's also a part of my anointing. How so? My giving has set the stage for me to be delivered from so many people in the

	past because I came to see that some people, once you bless them, start to feel entitled to your money, your possessions, and to you as a whole. They'll stop paying for their own lunches (if you allow them), and may even become lackadaisical with paying their bills, inwardly telling themselves that if they fall short, they can call you and get the money they need to catch up on their bills. Once you tell them "no" and you place a boundary around your money, they typically walk away offended, after all, bound people hate boundaries.
Witchcraft	There are many ways that witchcraft can serve or be used as a binder because there are two dimensions of witchcraft, with the first being flesh-established. The Bible tells us that witchcraft is a work of the flesh. However, it can and always does become spiritual as the practitioner grows increasingly determined to have his or her way. Therefore when dealing

with witchcraft of the flesh, people use manipulation, mind games, love-bombing, fear, intimidation, and seduction to accomplish their agendas, but once it crosses over into being a spiritual matter, practitioners will typically start engaging with New Age, crystals, sage, chakras, love spells, sex magic, and a lot of spiritual practices in an attempt to get their way. And, of course, both of these dimensions serve to connect the souls of people together, albeit illegally.

Debt	Proverbs 22:7 reads, "The rich ruleth over the poor, and the borrower is servant to the lender." Anytime, you owe money to a person, you are bound to that person; anytime, a person owes you money, that person is bound to you. This is why there are so many people who will always try to engage you financially. They are always wanting to borrow money or find some type of way to enter into a legal contract with you, thus allowing them

to bind themselves to you financially. Debt opens the door for unforgiveness, whereas someone whose financial face is void of God will always try to engage with you financially, and for a while, they will pay you back the money they've borrowed. Howbeit, over time, they will stop repaying you, thus making them indebted to you. In most cases, they will have no intentions of paying you back, so you'll have to do what the Bible says and forgive them, otherwise, the door you opened to them can be used by the enemy. After all, once unforgiveness entered the equation, that unforgiveness gives the enemy a key to your heart. This is why you don't loan money to everyone; this is why you turn your financial face away from some people because the moment they get access to that space, they will make you despise your gift of charity.

Agreement (Covenants, Contracts, Principles)

It goes without saying that one of the strongest binders is agreement, whether you agree on a political party or you've entered into a legal agreement (contract) with someone. According to Amos 3:3, two can only walk together if they are in agreement. Understand this—there are some people who form soul ties with other people by pretending to agree with them, and this isn't limited to the Eros or romantic realm. There are people who will attempt to bind themselves to you platonically by using something you're passionate about as a conversation piece, and pretending to agree with you. Once you grant them access into your life, they'll immediately start looking for something the two of you agree about, as well as an area of your life where there is darkness (ignorance). This is how they start bringing you into submission to their will. Additionally, there are agreements formed in the realm of the spirit between our parents and forefathers that we have to address, otherwise, their demons will become our demons, and the debts they owed will fall upon our heads. This is why these ties have to be broken; they shouldn't be ignored or minimized. They have to be addressed because they can open doors for the wrong people to enter into our lives.

Jealousy

Jealousy is a binder, whereas it provokes the individual with the evil heart to obsess over another person or a group of people. If someone is jealous of you, you won't make a move that they are not interested in. So, while they may block you on social media, a jealous soul will create a profile under a false name just to monitor your profile. This particular binder causes its host to hear the voices of demons saying, for example, "She thinks she's better than everyone" or "She thinks she's cute!" It can get so bad that the host of this foul spirit can monitor a

	person for so long that they can easily mimic the person's voice, patterns and mannerisms; they also become pretty skilled at knowing the person's "type". This binder opens the door for bitterness, hatred, and witchcraft to repeatedly attack the victim by provoking the victim's assailant with evil thoughts; this way, the host will repeatedly speak word curses at or about the other party.
Envy	Like its evil cousin, jealousy, envy is a binding agent as well; people can and do bind themselves to other people through envy. Unlike jealousy, envy wears a mask; people bound by this issue and spirit are usually obsessed with the people they are envious of, and will seek to help them before hindering them. Their goal is to learn as much as they can about the objects of their obsessions so they can mirror and mimic those behaviors. Doing this requires that they offer up a measure of kindness, vulnerability, and self-

sacrifice. This is why most of the people who are attacked by envy are often caught off guard or they may have trouble forgiving themselves, often saying aloud, "I knew something was off about that girl!" Nevertheless, they were so put off by the flattery, the gifts, and the stories that the other parties shared with them that they started gaslighting themselves, telling themselves that the other party, while weird, was just trying to be nice. Nevertheless, the person was creating a soul tie for the purpose of siphoning their anointing and their stuff; the envious souls went out of their way to steal those people's destinies.

It goes without saying that there are many binders out there; these binders set the stage for the bonds that people will attempt to formulate with you. This is why you have to be both careful and prayerful. Never get distracted or lower your guard just because you're being love-bombed, flattered, or placed on a pedestal. And don't let a gift set the stage for your fall or your demise.

- **Proverbs 23:6-8:** Eat thou not the bread of him that hath an evil eye, neither desire thou his dainty meats: For as he thinketh in his heart, so is he: Eat and drink, saith he to thee; but his heart is not with thee. The morsel which thou hast eaten shalt thou vomit up, and lose thy sweet words.

As a reminder, whatever attracts you can bind you. So, if someone is financially attracted to you, that person can end up soul-tying himself or herself to the side of you that deals with money. Furthermore, you can resist this particular type of soul tie by refusing to:

1. Give the individual money.
2. Give the individual access to any information that relates to your finances like yearly earnings, debt information, or any form of financial information.
3. Take their money.
4. Co-sign on a loan, lease, or any type of debt with the individual.
5. Allow them to communicate with that side of you.

This is done by keeping your answers short and to the point, changing the subject, and drawing boundaries around certain topics. It may sound like, "Brad, this is the third time you've asked me how much money I make in a year. I don't care to share this with you, so let's talk about something else. What do you like to do for fun?" After this, you do not have to explain why you don't want to share the info with Brad. Your job is to point out the problem, and then present a solution.

In this, what you're doing is spinning around and showing them the face that you want them to see, and not the face they want to see. What you've likely discovered over time is that some people will start a conversation about one subject, just to use that conversation as a passageway to another discussion. You don't have to allow this behavior unless you want to. It's a form of manipulation, and you don't want to normalize this in any of your relationships.

RED FLAGS & RED LIGHTS

> There hath no temptation taken you but such as is common
> to man: but God is faithful, who will not suffer you to be
> tempted above that ye are able; but will with the temptation
> also make a way to escape, that ye may be able to bear it.
> 1 Corinthians 10:13

Red light, green light—stop! I can't say that this was my
favorite game when I was a kid, but I didn't mind playing
it. What kept this game from being at the top of my list
was the repetitiveness of it. Don't get me wrong. I've
played many games that involved repetition, but I played
those games when I was in a mellow mood. This is
because I was a super adventurous hyperactive soul with
a need to bleed. No, I'm not saying that I was devious or
that I intentionally harmed myself. I am saying that I
climbed trees, ran races, chased people with insects,
picked up frogs, fished for crayfish with makeshift
fishing poles—that kinda stuff. If having fun meant I
had to scrape my knee or get a mild concussion, I was
down for it. I was a girly tomboy, if that makes any bit
of sense. I loved dolls, fashion, and beauty trends; I

loved all-things-girly, but I also loved doing silly things like digging holes in the backyard to find and catch earthworms, wandering off into tall weeds just to catch an unsuspecting grasshopper, squatting at the edge of a small lake with a bucket while waiting on a minnow to appear, and writing horror books using my notebook paper. So, I wasn't an enemy of repetition, but I wasn't a fan of it either. I simply learned to feel my way through the day.

Repetition. That's a word that we should know all too well because, as humans, we tend to be creatures of habit, constantly making the same mistakes over and over again. We date the same demons in different folks all the time, and every time we run into those demons behind unfamiliar faces, we give them another pass. That's, of course, if we like the skin-suits they've decided to disguise themselves with. The Bible says it in 1 Samuel 16:7 this way, "But the Lord said unto Samuel, Look not on his countenance, or on the height of his stature; because I have refused him: for the Lord seeth not as man seeth; for man looketh on the outward appearance, but the Lord looketh on the heart." How many times have we accepted people who God has rejected simply because we were looking at the skin they were wrapped in? Here's what I noticed. Demons have patterns, and get this, you can easily identify the type of demon by its pattern (in many cases). For example, someone love-bombing you, moving way too fast in their relationship with you, and putting you on punishment (cold shoulder, ignored calls, threatening to cut you off) whenever they don't get their way is probably a narcissist or an incredibly narcissistic individual. In other words, the individual is likely bound by the Jezebel spirit. A prideful, egotistical soul who keeps twisting your words and misunderstanding you is likely bound by the spirit of Leviathan. Knowing each demon's patterns, traits, and nuisances makes it easier for you to identify and avoid them. As a reminder—you can't talk a demon out of being a demon. In other words, pointing out to the person in front of you that they need deliverance, and their demons likely came in because their fathers abandoned them, their mothers had a rotating door of men, and because their ex-spouses cheated and deserted them is not going to make them reevaluate their lives and repent. No, you'll simply start another argument and spend another day moping around, feeling sorry for yourself. "Give not that which is holy unto the dogs, neither cast ye your pearls before swine, lest they trample them under their feet, and turn again and rend you" (Matthew 7:6).

But we're not going to talk about demonic traits; instead, in this chapter, we are going to focus on three red flags to look out for, and three altars that every believer should have in their lives before they even consider inviting someone into their lives romantically. The first three we'll discuss are the red flags; they are:

1. Generalization
2. Abdication/Subjectification
3. Objectification

These three make up the three dimensions of extreme trauma. Everything has a spectrum: good versus evil, bad versus good, darkness versus light, up versus down, right versus left—you get the point. But within a spectrum, you will find sub-spectrums. For example, if someone made it to the furthest end on this particular spectrum, there would be degrees. Think about the spectrum of narcissism; there are narcissistic people, just as there are people who are narcissists, meaning they are on the far right or left of the spectrum. A better example is good versus evil. Matthew 12:43-45 demonstrates this principle; it reads, "When the unclean spirit is gone out of a man, he walketh through dry places, seeking rest, and findeth none. Then he saith, I will return into my house from whence I came out; and when he is come, he findeth it empty, swept, and garnished. Then goeth he, and taketh with himself seven other spirits more wicked than himself, and they enter in and dwell there: and the last state of that man is worse than the first." Notice in this scripture, there is a mention of seven spirits *more wicked* than the one that was originally cast out. So, on the spectrum of good and evil, we could crop out the evil side, and on the evil side, there are demons (and people) who are wicked, but there are demons (and people) who are far more wicked than the ones on the left. This is important because, as believers, we need to understand that if we don't repent, study the Word, and if we continue on the paths that repeatedly lead us astray, the cases that Satan, the accuser, files against us in the spirit realm will be escalated.

Generalization

Statements like ···

> "All men cheat."
>
> "Today's women are masculine."
>
> "Black men are lazy."
>
> "White men are racist."
>
> "Black children are fatherless."
>
> "Black women are angry."
>
> "White women are Karens."

··· are all forms of prejudice; another way of saying this is—these are generalizations. The word "generalization" comes from the word "generalize," and according to Merriam Webster, it means "to derive or induce (a general conception or principle) from particulars; to draw a general conclusion from." Generalization, at its base, is nothing but lazy discernment. It happens when we take a situation that we've been in, and allow the trauma, the hurt, the rejection, the guilt, and the shame from that situation to become our bullies. This is when we start developing what is known today as "triggers." Plainly put, your trigger is nothing but a demonic doorbell. Just like we knock on doors and ring doorbells to see if anyone's home or to see who's home, demons and demonized people will "push your buttons" to get a reaction out of you. The goal is to get your demons to answer or react; that is if you're demonically bound. Secondly, the objective is to see what demons you're bound by. So, if you're bound by unclean spirits, they will typically surface to address the situation. No, they are not doing this to protect you; they are doing this to protect their investment and to see what demons are trying to have some face-time with them. Yes, demons like to forge partnerships or networks with other demons, and yes, some demons aren't interested in forming partnerships with one another. Don't get me wrong—the kingdom of darkness is not divided against itself, but like angels, demons are oftentimes assigned to people, and if David's demons don't see any benefit in connecting with Mandy's demons, there will be no chemistry between the two. Again, Mandy may end up forming a one-sided soul tie with David, constantly calling and obsessing over him, but David won't soul-tie himself to her unless he sees a benefit in their connection. He may sexually soul tie himself to her, but he'll avoid her in so many other ways.

Generalization is a form of trauma; it is a trauma response, and it typically involves general thoughts and statements about a group of people based on our family's history, fear, ignorance, media, and experiences with one or more people from that specific group, etc. The reason this is dangerous is because people who fall into the trap of generalization are blinded by unforgiveness, trauma, and ignorance. So, if you dated a man who generalized women, he may be the nicest guy in the beginning, but over time, you'll meet one of his many dark faces. For example, when he's happy with you, he might refer to you using pet names like baby, sweetheart, beautiful lady, sweetie, honey drop, etc. However, when he's offended, he may then revert to using your first name. So, if your name is Kathy, he may say, "Kathy, have you seen my watch?!" When he's incredibly angry, this is when he'll bear his heart, and say things like, "You women are all the same!" He may even say, "My Mom told me to stop falling in love so fast, but I didn't listen! Now, look at me—in the house with another gold-digging Jezebel who doesn't care about me!" Because of his unhealed trauma, it is impossible for him to love another human being. He can experience heightened emotions, obsession, dependency, codependency, fear of being alone, fear of being without the individual in question, territorialism, the fear of change, etc. All of these issues look and feel like love to someone who has never experienced it. And typically when people reach this stage of hurt and trauma, they can be rather abusive—emotionally, verbally, and sometimes physically. So, while they may be nice people when they're calm, they can be both dark and dangerous when they're upset. This is a huge red flag. Anyone who generalizes a group of people should be avoided at all costs. If you entertain the person, you will soon discover that the group of people he or she has generalized is the same group of people he or she is obsessed with.

Abdication/Subjectification

I put these on the same pointer because they are on the same spectrum, one to the far right and the other to the far left. Let's look at the definitions of their base words.

275

Abdicate (Oxford Languages):

- (of a monarch) renounce one's throne.
- fail to fulfill or undertake (a responsibility or duty).

Ephesians 4:26 reads, "And hath raised us up together, and made us sit together in heavenly places in Christ Jesus." We all have ranks, positions, and responsibilities that have been assigned to us by the Most High God, and we have been graced (empowered) to carry out those duties. This empowerment is what we refer to as the anointing, but we are also spirits living inside of bodies. We are like pigs in a blanket who haven't been slaughtered or cooked just yet. We might be wrapped in flesh, but we are still alive, trying to avoid a devil who, like a roaring lion, is going about seeking who he may devour (see 1 Peter 5:8).

We've gone through our fair share of hurt and shame, and I think I speak for the masses when I say—we all want to rest and enjoy our lives without evil being a part of it. But we have an assignment; we have a path that we are supposed to be on, and truth be told, the enemy is always on the outskirts of that path whispering, shouting, begging, and trying to seduce us outside of

God's will. And sometimes, we get weary. Sometimes, we get lonely. Sometimes, we get bored. At other times, we get overwhelmed with it all, and that's when Satan's voice starts to echo in our heads. He speaks to us a lot when we're tired, hungry, lonely, or frustrated. He then offers us happiness in place of joy, quick results in place of patience, lust in place of love, relief from his attacks in place of peace, niceness in place of kindness, good works in place of goodness, comfort in place of faithfulness, technology in place of gentleness, and a few diagnoses in place of self-control. No, I'm not against people being diagnosed with an issue. In this, I'm saying that Satan will hand you alternatives to the paths God wants you to be on and the seeds He wants you to plant. In this, he tries to get us to abdicate our seats of authority; he tries to get us to become passive as it relates to our destinies and assignments. In this, many people surrender their authority to their demonized partners, their controlling friends, or to sin altogether. Slowly, but surely, they begin to abdicate their seats of authority by exchanging their identities for costumes that the world celebrates. Note: your God-given authority is directly linked to your authenticity.

This is to say that the world, if allowed, would "ahab" you, meaning they'd rob you of your authority and toss you into bondage.

Conclusion: avoid people who are too fearful to walk in their authority because, chances are, they are bound by the Ahab spirit, and wherever you find Ahab, there's a Jezebel with the deed to the individual nearby. Whether that Jezebel is his or her mother, an ex, or their community, an ahab'ed soul is not free to marry, so the only role that will be open to you will be that of a concubine or a eunuch. Ahab can't cleave to anyone because he is married to Jezebel in the realm of the spirit.

Subject (Oxford Languages):
- cause or force to undergo (a particular experience of form of treatment).
- bring (a person or country) under one's control or jurisdiction, typically by using force.

Subjectification is simply subjecting others to a group of principles with the intent of bringing them under your control. There are two types of control; they are covert control and overt control. People who lack self-control typically specialize in people-control. What does the Bible say about these types of souls? Proverbs 25:28 reads, "He that hath no rule over his own spirit is like a city that is broken down, and without walls." A city that has no walls is open for attack; there is no boundary in place to keep the enemy out, which means that the city in question has been overtaken. So, a person who has no rule over his own spirit will have a demonic ruler, and please understand that demons think in numbers and in generations. This is to say they won't be satisfied with the host that they've overtaken. No, they will use that person to gather more souls; this is when we start to see promiscuity, fear tactics, and even people going back to school and chasing the highest degrees, not to better themselves, but to put themselves in a position to control, intimidate and dominate more people, especially people of high rank. After all, according to Ephesians 6:12, "For we wrestle not against flesh and blood, but against principalities, against powers, against the rulers of the darkness of this world, against spiritual wickedness in high places." I can't tell you how many unhealthy, demonized people I've come across who have or are chasing doctorate degrees or other high-level degrees, and they genuinely believe their titles entitle them to access to other people, especially people of power and notoriety. Don't get me wrong; there are many healthy, non-narcissistic people out there who are doctors, in doctorate programs, or are ascending the ranks in other areas, but this doesn't overshadow the fact that there are a lot of broken souls out there running after power and platforms. And one thing about the Jezebel spirit is it seeks to control people in positions of influence. You see, Jezebel doesn't have to give any commands to the crowd if she has a puppet named Ahab to do her bidding. In other words, she doesn't have to be the puppet if she can be the puppet's master.

Subjectification is another form or expression of high trauma. If you meet someone who controls other people, either passively or assertively, do not connect with that person in any shape, form, or fashion. A sign, for example, that they specialize in covert control would be this—they are living in the house with someone bound by the Jezebel spirit, and while they complain about being bullied, abused, and ostracized by that person, they refuse to move because the rent is free or cheap for them. Ask any psychologist, psychiatrist, deliverance minister, or anyone who's had to hear this story time and time again—most (not all) people who stay with Jezebel year after year tend to become relatively narcissistic themselves, vying for power over the Jezebel that controls them because they want to enjoy the benefits of Jezebel without the abuse, control, and the mind games. They will typically go from Jezebel to Jezebel, only leaving their mother's house or whomever it is that has the Jezebel spirit when they find somebody who's willing to couch them or let them move in. When they reach out for therapy or deliverance, they are not truly seeking to be free of Jezebel, they want tactics and tools to help them manage and control the narcissistic individual. Again, this is because the spirit of Jezebel intentionally makes them rely on others; this is a form of idolatry. This is how the devil becomes their dealer. They become too afraid to live on their own, pay their own bills, or buy something for themselves in their own names, so they will tolerate Jezebel to get the benefits. In this, they don't realize that Jezebel is teaching them to be Jezebel while they are under that spirit's control.

281

Again, I'm not saying this is true for every person who's living with and relying on a narcissist, but most people who've been relying on a narcissist for years tend to behave like the people they complain about, albeit covertly.

In short, the Bible tells us to test the spirit in 1 John 4:1; it reads, "Beloved, believe not every spirit, but try the spirits whether they are of God: because many false prophets are gone out into the world." How do you try (test) a spirit? Matthew 7:16 answers this question. "Ye shall know them by their fruits. Do men gather grapes of thorns, or figs of thistles?" But what fruits is this scripture talking about? The fruits of the Spirit, of course! Galatians 5:22-23 reads, "But the fruit of the Spirit is love, joy, peace, long-suffering, gentleness, goodness, faith, meekness, temperance: against such there is no law." Other fruits include the works of the flesh; these are the issues that spring from unguarded hearts. Galatians 5:19-21 reads, "Now the works of the flesh are manifest, which are these; adultery, fornication, uncleanness, lasciviousness, idolatry, witchcraft, hatred, variance, emulations, wrath, strife, seditions, heresies,envyings, murders, drunkenness, revelings, and such like: of the which I tell you before, as I have also told you in time past, that they which do such things shall not inherit the kingdom of God." So, your objective is to pray and pay attention to the fruits they produce, but you can't do this until you aren't blinded by your own issues. Matthew 7:3-5 instructs us with, "And why beholdest thou the mote that is in thy brother's eye, but considerest not the beam that is in thine own eye? Or how wilt thou say to thy brother, Let me pull out the mote out of thine eye; and, behold, a beam is in thine own eye? Thou hypocrite, first cast out the beam out of thine own eye; and then shalt thou see clearly to cast out the mote out of thy brother's eye."

This is to say beware of people who:
- Control or attempt to control other people covertly or overtly.
- Control or attempt to control you covertly or overtly.
- Can't take no for an answer.
- Are unteachable and can't take correction.
- Hate authority and authority figures.
- Have emotional tantrums or put you on punishment when they don't get their way.

- Try to drive other people out of your life.
- Require a sin offering to be with you or stay with you.
- Routinely or regularly play the victim.
- Create chaotic situations, disappear, and then reappear and try to rescue you from the mess they've created.

Objectification

This is the worst type of trauma response that a human can have. What is objectification? Its base word is "objectify," and according to Oxford Languages, it means:

1. Degrade to the status of a mere object.

Crazily enough, this is what serial killers do. They view other human beings as objects; this helps them to carry out their crimes with no guilt or remorse. In Matthew 24, Jesus talked about the last days, and in verse 12, He spoke of one of the issues that would be prevalent at that time. It reads, "And because iniquity shall abound, the love of many shall wax cold." He's saying that many people will become cold-hearted or, better yet, their love will pass away; yes, even while they are still alive. In this, He is talking about narcissism. E Medicine Health reports the following:

"Narcissistic personality disorder (narcissism) is a psychiatric disorder characterized by a pattern of self-importance (grandiosity), a constant need for admiration and attention, and a lack of empathy for others. Because of this lack of empathy, a narcissist cannot really love you. Narcissists do not experience and show love in the sense that most people do" (Source: emedicinehealth.com/Can A Narcissist Really Love You?/John P. Cunha, DO, FACOEP).

Read this carefully. There are levels of evil, and when a person's trauma, demons, and their choices lead them to objectify other humans, that person becomes beyond dangerous. In many cases, they can easily be diagnosed as psychopathic or sociopathic. Understand this—James can be bound by Jezebel spirit, but his next door neighbor, Brad, may have the Jezebel spirit too. However, the one that's in Brad may be far more wicked than the one that's in James. And this is what the spirit of Jezebel does; it sees and treats people as mere objects. This is to say never date or tolerate people who:

1. Dislike or hate God.
2. Dislike or hate themselves.
3. Generalize others.
4. Don't respect others.
5. Are more interested in your body than they are in your mind.

What makes objectification so dangerous? For one, it causes the person struggling with it to dehumanize other people. In this, it prohibits the individual from loving others, and where there is no love, there will be no grace. Next, it ushers in hatred, and hatred in its infant stages, may show up as disdain. In this, everything that you do may aggravate the individual who's struggling with early-stage objectification. This aggravation may look like:

- The individual in question getting increasingly agitated by the way you chew your food.
- The individual in question becoming visibly annoyed anytime you enter a room or come within a certain feet of them.

- The individual in question criticizing everything that you do; it would seem that you can't do anything right.
- The individual in question refusing to have deep, heart-to-heart conversations with you, preferring to keep all of your conversations surface-level.
- The individual in question cutting you out of their plans.

Objectification can and often looks like:
- The individual in question only treating you well when they want something.
- The individual in question constantly asking you for favors, but getting aggravated when you say no or whenever you ask them for a favor in return.
- If you're sexually active with the individual, he or she may start to perform degrading acts or request sexual favors that you deem to be demeaning, humiliating, and dehumanizing.
- Volunteering you to do favors for others without your permission. For example, a wife who hates her husband may tell her brother that her husband can come and help him and his wife move from their old home to their new one. "No need to hire a

moving truck," she says. "Freddie can do all of that by himself! He needs the exercise anyway."

- Viewing your possessions and resources as their own, all the while guarding their belongings from you—even stuff they've stolen from you.

Someone who objectifies others is a killer in the making. Sure, they may never go as far to take a life, but they will seek to destroy you in any way possible, starting with your self-esteem and potentially ending with your reputation.

The reason this topic is important when dealing with soul ties is because every year, our news feeds are buzzing with stories of people being killed by their romantic partners, and get this, most, if not all, of these incidents could have been avoided, but we tend to ignore the red flags in favor of what we want to believe about our love interests. The Bureau of Justice Statistics reports the following:

"Of the estimated 4,970 female victims of murder and non-negligent manslaughter in 2021, data reported by law enforcement agencies indicate

that 34% were killed by an intimate partner
(figure 1). By comparison, about 6% of the 17,970
males murdered that year were victims of intimate
partner homicide.

Overall, 76% of female murders and 56% of male
murders were perpetrated by someone known to
the victim. About 16% of female murder victims
were killed by a no intimate family member—
parent, grandparent, sibling, in-law, and other
family member—compared to 10% of male murder
victims.

A larger percentage of males (21%) were murdered
by a stranger than females (12%). For 1 out of
every 3 male murder victims and 1 out of every 5
female murder victims, the relationship between
the victim and the offender was unknown"
(Source: Bureau of Justice Statistics/Female
Murder Victims and Victim-Offender Relationship,
2021/Erica L. Smith, BJS Statistician).

Hear me—no one (not a single soul) intentionally kills
someone they love. People kill who they are obsessed
with and don't feel good enough to have. You see, God is

love, and when we love God, we put Him first. This is what increases His presence in us; this is what teaches and empowers us to love others. However, where God isn't, something dark will be. It will sit in that dark void and disguise itself as an angel of light, infesting the hosts' mind with all types of evil ideas and offenses. If the host does not cast down the imaginations, have those much needed and hard conversations, get therapy,or pray about the situation, he or she will come into agreement with the dark entity, and this is when that devil will start to merge its personality with the host's. Before long, what was once a series of evil thoughts can and will turn into a chorus of evil voices coming from within. In other words, the host will be in need of deliverance. That's when the demon will start repeatedly and even randomly tormenting its host day and night, making its host restless, angry, and eventually desperate to make the tormenting thoughts stop. This is where and when the spirit of murder comes on the scene, promising the infected soul relief should he or she take the life of the other party or take his or her own life. Mark 12:29-31 reads, "And Jesus answered him, The first of all the commandments is, Hear, O Israel;

The Lord our God is one Lord: And thou shalt love the Lord thy God with all thy heart, and with all thy soul, and with all thy mind, and with all thy strength: this is the first commandment. And the second is like, namely this, Thou shalt love thy neighbor as thyself. There is none other commandment greater than these." In this text, we find Jesus saying, "Thou shalt love thy neighbor as thyself." So, what we can gather from this is the three-fold cord of love. We must:

1. Love God with every part of our being.
2. Love ourselves.
3. Love our neighbors in the same manner or in the same measure in which we love ourselves.

Simply put, don't ignore the red flags. Objectification isn't something you should overlook; instead, when and if you see it in a person, run for your life, after all, objectification is the heartbeat of:

- Drug dealers.
- Drug addicts.
- Serial killers.
- Prostitutes and pimps.
- Religious people.

- (Some) politicians.
- Demons.

From Breakup to Breakdown to Breakthrough

> For his anger endureth but a moment; in his favor is life:
> weeping may endure for a night, but joy cometh in the
> morning.
> Psalm 30:5

I remember the Lord repeatedly dealing with me about an old friend of mine. Our friendship had become our snare. We'd been friends for a very long time, and we'd come to rely on each other so much that our covenant had formed a coven of sorts. Don't get me wrong—we weren't witches, but we'd learned to cling to one another, fearing what life would look like on the other side of change. She feared losing me as a friend, and I feared losing her, so we spent exorbitant amounts of time on the phone talking about absolutely nothing. We no longer agreed with one another about most things except the fact that Jesus Christ is Lord. I was progressively chasing God, wanting to know more about Him, but she was more of a traditional Christian, comfortable with what she already knew about Him. My conversations were progressive, but she spoke mostly about the past, constantly talking about high school, exes, and revisiting old wounds. She wasn't a bad person; I eventually learned that bad people and bound people tend to commit the same crimes. We were both bound, but I was on my way out of a season that she'd committed herself to. You see, a season is more than a block of time that we find ourselves in; a season is the space of time that we spend, serve, or are committed to a mindset.

- **Spent Time:** This deals with our will; this is what we choose to do with our time.

- **Served Time:** This is a time when we are locked in a principle or a series of principles as a result of a generational curse, contract, altar, or sin. It is a sentence given to us by God, and oftentimes imposed upon us by both angels and demons. How so? An angel's job is to protect us by guarding some of the doors that we would seek to enter into or exit from out of ignorance, ambition, fear, or demonic temptation. These doors aren't always permanently closed to us; oftentimes, they are temporarily (seasonally) closed to us. So, when we move towards the edge of a season that we've been sentenced to, we enter into a dimension called "grace." This happens when we venture to the outskirts of our realms (realities) in our pursuit of God, but when we venture out due to ungodly ambition or fear, we enter into the dimension of "mercy." Grace is unmerited or undeserved favor, whereas mercy is God withholding or protecting us from the punishment or judgments that we actually deserve. A demon's job, on the other hand, is to lead us outside of God's boundaries so that we can be legally bound. Both angels and demons are legalistic because the spirit realm is run by legalities.

- **Committed Time:** This is the time when God turns you over to a system or a set of principles. The difference between served time and committed time is this—served time has a time stamp, but committed time can only be overturned by an external agent, typically an intercessor when it is unfavorable. "And even as they did not like to retain God in their knowledge, God gave them over to a reprobate mind, to do those things which are

295

not convenient" (Romans 8:28). Also consider 1 Corinthians 5:5, which reads, "Hand this man over to Satan for the destruction of the flesh, so that his spirit may be saved on the day of the Lord." Lastly, another perfect example of committed time can be found in Jesus' proclamation regarding the Church of Thyatira, which reads, "And unto the angel of the church in Thyatira write; These things saith the Son of God, who hath his eyes like unto a flame of fire, and his feet are like fine brass; I know thy works, and charity, and service, and faith, and thy patience, and thy works; and the last to be more than the first. Notwithstanding I have a few things against thee, because thou sufferest that woman Jezebel, which calleth herself a prophetess, to teach and to seduce my servants to commit fornication, and to eat things sacrificed unto idols. And I gave her space to repent of her fornication; and she repented not. Behold, I will cast her into a bed, and them that commit adultery with her into great tribulation, except they repent of their deeds. And I will kill her children with death; and all the churches shall know that I am he which searcheth the reins and hearts: and I will give unto every one of you according to your work" (see Revelation 2:18-23).

Committed time is oftentimes permanent, and just as it can be unfavorable, it can also be favorable. For example, God committed the Israelites to the Promised Land, but just like an intercessor can help to rescue someone from a sentence (consider Abraham rescuing Lot through intercession), the devil can send a binding agent to ensnare a favored soul and lead them away from favor to bondage. This is why Apostle Paul warned the church in Galatians 5:1 this way, "Stand fast therefore in the liberty wherewith Christ hath made us free, and be not entangled again with the yoke of bondage." Notice he used the word "again." Throughout the Bible, we've witnessed the Israelites get themselves entangled *again* and *again* until God finally declared in Jeremiah 3:8, "And I saw, when for all the causes whereby backsliding Israel committed adultery I had put her away, and given her a bill of divorce; yet her treacherous sister Judah feared not, but went and played the harlot also."

There are other seasons that we can find ourselves in. They include, but are not limited to:

- **Expected End:** Healing is an expectation, deliverance is an expectation, joy is an expectation, but they are not one-time events; they are on a continuum, meaning they are committed times, even though we can venture outside of God's will and pick up more devils, more issues, and more things to cry about, we can also turn back to God and take advantage of Jesus' work on the cross; that is if we truly repent from the heart and not just from the head.

- **Due Season:** This is the space of time in revelation that allows and empowers us to reap what we've sown. Again, this isn't just a block of time, it's a space of grace and favor when the fear of failure lifts, along with the writer's block, the lack of energy, and all of the noise surrounding us suddenly stills itself, thus allowing us to better hear what the Lord is saying. This is a time of jubilee, a time to rejoice, and the space to do so.

It is also important to note that a season and a time are not one and the same. While seasons are divided into time slots, a time is not the totality of a season. For example, most people put failure and success on the same spectrum, with failure serving as the nemesis of success, but this is an error. Failure is not the opposite of success, it is the skeleton of success. It creates the structure by which we succeed. This is why Proverbs 24:16 states, "For a just man falleth seven times, and riseth up again: but the wicked shall fall into mischief." Is failure a prerequisite of success? Not if you're Jesus, but if you aren't our Lord and Savior, the answer is yes. Nothing in the Heavens or the Earth can be sustained without respect and honor; whatever you don't respect or honor, you stand to lose. So, to teach you to succeed, God allows you to fail; this is His way of preparing you to succeed. Show me a man or a woman in the Bible who has succeeded without failing, and I'll show you Jesus. Understand this—to fail, according to Oxford Languages, is defined as:

- be unsuccessful in achieving one's goal.
- neglect to do something.

Here's the thing. God gives us an idea; we implement our

own plans into His idea, or we allow the enemy of our souls to entice us with a good idea in an attempt to distract us from the God idea. And that's when failure happens. So, we succeed in bringing to pass what God wanted us to bring to pass, but we fail when we put fear, worldliness, and selfish ambition in the mix. Sure, we can end up creating something that's ingenious, but we'll fail at creating what God wanted us to create— however this is just a part of the design itself. We simply learn to succeed by failing.

So, a small space of time and the events that take place in that window of time are not considered seasons individually, but they make up the seasons that we're in. Let me explain. Notice that the words "real, realm, and reality" are almost the same. What's real to you determines your reality. A realm is a kingdom. A kingdom is ran by principles; it has laws, rules, norms, ethics, and regulations. It also has officers that enforce the laws. So, you and I are both a part of God's Kingdom (if you're saved). But just because we're citizens there doesn't necessarily mean that we live there. For example, I was a citizen of America living in Germany at one space in time.

Had I committed a crime in Germany, the German government would have had the legal right (in their country) to arrest and imprison me. Similarly, a Christian living outside the will of God can be legally bound by demons. This is why deliverance isn't always the answer to a demonically bound soul; sometimes, the individual needs to repent and return to God's will. This is evidenced in James 4:7, which reads, "Submit yourselves therefore to God. Resist the devil, and he will flee from you." And get this—the United States has an extradition treaty with Germany, so had I committed a crime there before returning to the States, because of the treaty which, of course, is a legality, the United States government would have turned me over to the German officials. We have to understand that the same is true when dealing with the spirit world. If you sin against Heaven, and then rush back to church in an attempt to blur out the sin, the devil still has a legal right to come into the church and bind you. This is why the ministry of deliverance will continue to flourish as long as this Earth floats between the stars. Repentance doesn't always destroy the devil's legal rights to a person, especially if the individual is still holding onto the stuff that they accumulated or got while in darkness (i.e. the gifts your former sex partners gave you, anger, unforgiveness, beliefs, proclamations and declarations, sex toys, etc.). Sometimes, you have to fast AND pray. All the same, you have to be willing to go without the television set, the soiled mattress (that doubled as an altar when you sacrificed your body on it for someone you weren't married to), and your newfound belief that "all men cheat" or "all women are gold diggers." Understand that most seasons are sentences (time spent in a mindset), but every sentence ends with a period. Every sentence forms a complete statement, but a sentence is not finished until it is finalized with a period. If you place a comma where God wanted to place a period, you will continue to write the same story, all the while introducing new characters to the mix; this is called a stronghold. It is a season on repeat; a network of cycles that are in automation. To end a season, there has to be a breakup, and no, I'm not just talking about a breakup between two individuals. I'm talking about a breakup between you and a set of principles. As a matter of fact, you can't end a soul tie without doing just this. At the beginning of this chapter, I mentioned an old friend and how God called me out of that friendship. I can remember going before God in prayer and saying something along the lines of, "I don't know how to let her go. She's been my friend for well over twenty years." I didn't understand God's declaration about Him closing that door. I thought I needed to "do" something when, in truth, He was instructing me to "become" someone different. He responded and let me know that my assignment was simple—let the Word do a good work in me. I simply needed to study His Word all the more, and I had to stop resisting His instructions whenever they didn't make sense to me. He helped me to identify our binder. With this friend, our binder was trauma. She'd seen me through a lot, and I'd seen her through a lot. For years, I'd unconsciously allowed her to dominate our conversations, talking nonstop about her past, my past, and the day we were in. I don't remember us talking too much about tomorrow outside of our talks of our future husbands. God laid one simple set of instructions on my heart. I had to stop being a listening ear. I had to use my voice. So, I made God a promise. I would stop listening to her complain incessantly about everything and everyone. In my mind, I didn't think this would end the friendship. I genuinely thought that it would help her to change her ways; this way, God would change her mind. After she started her ritual of complaining, I stopped her mid-sentence and told her that God has been far too God to her for her to complain the way she does. I told her that I'd promised God that I was no longer going to sit there and listen to her complain anymore. What was I doing? Unbeknownst to me, I was ripping off the identity she'd given me, and with that identity, I was rejecting the role she'd assigned me to in her life. After I was done speaking, she humbly agreed—God had truly been far too good to her for her to complain the way she did. After that, she started becoming more mindful of what she said, but the issue was a stronghold, so she kept defaulting to it, and I'd cut her off and remind her of our agreement. Not long after this, we went from talking everyday, several times a day for hours on end to speaking every other day for a few minutes. I kept enforcing the new rule, hoping that she'd break the habit, but instead, this didn't happen. We then started talking every few days to a week, speaking only for 15-30 minutes at a time. Slowly, but surely we talked more infrequently, and when we did speak, we didn't talk for long because the only thing we had in common at that point was Jesus. She wasn't bad; we were both bound, and again, I was chasing God, which is synonymous with chasing freedom. So, to break a soul tie, you have to break up with the principles that align you with the other party, reminding yourself that two can only walk together if they are in agreement (see Amos 3:3). Sometimes, the binder is gossip. Sometimes, the binder is the past and your refusal to let go of it. Sometimes, the binder is an old ungodly principle that has managed to creep into many minority communities, and that is familial foolishness. Most of us have heard our families say, "When everyone else forsakes you, you will always have family." This belief has allowed and encouraged us to tolerate toxic, ungodly, and traumatic behaviors from our family members, all the while allowing the generational curses in our bloodlines to groom our children while they are still in our care. What we normalize to them gets passed on from us to them, and ultimately to their children and their children's children.

To breakup with a principle, you have to study and show yourself approved (see 2 Timothy 7:15). In this, the old principles and beliefs have to be called what they are—lies and deception. This will cause your subconscious mind to dislodge the information from your heart and place it back in the waiting room (conscious). From there, you have to usher the truth in; this is what sets the stage for your freedom from both demons and strongholds. Remember, John 8:32 says, "And ye shall know the truth, and the truth shall make you free." But knowing the truth isn't enough, after all, knowledge puffs us up (see 1 Corinthians 8:1). You need to understand the truth. "Wisdom is the principal thing; therefore get wisdom: and with all thy getting get understanding" (Proverbs 4:7).

Next, you need wisdom. Where do you find wisdom? James 3:17 answers this question. It reads, "But the wisdom from above is first pure, then peaceable, gentle, open to reason, full of mercy and good fruits, impartial and sincere." Proverbs 2:6 states, "For the Lord gives wisdom; from his mouth come knowledge and understanding." Wisdom comes from God, but get this—He doesn't always drop it from Heaven to your head. He places it in earthen vessels.

- **Proverbs 24:6:** For by wise counsel thou shalt make thy war: and in multitude of counselors there is safety.

- **Proverbs 20:8:** Plans are established by counsel; by wise guidance wage war.

- **Proverbs 12:15:** The way of a fool is right in his own eyes, but a wise man listens to advice.

- **Proverbs 11:14:** Where no counsel is, the people fall: but in the multitude of counselors there is safety.

- **Proverbs 19:20-21:** Hear counsel, and receive instruction, that thou mayest be wise in thy latter end. There are many devices in a man's heart; nevertheless the counsel of the LORD, that shall stand.

Here's what I've learned and experienced. It is rare to come across believers who truly want wise counsel; they want wise counselors so they can dumb them down. People look for wise counselors these days because they want to argue their points, hoping to find people who have God's heart to understand their hearts. This is just the enemy's way of still trying to try a case that he's already lost. And when their wise counselors hold onto wisdom, and stand firm on the Word of God, many believers today then take to social media to call themselves victims. They don't want to break up with the ungodly principles that have allowed the same principalities that have ruled over their bloodlines to rule over them and their households. Satan has convinced a lot of people that it is God who needs to change His mind, rather than them needing to change their ways.

And finally, to breakup with ungodly, demonic, and perverse principles, you have to be willing to let people mislabel you, misjudge you, and ultimately fall away from you when you don't adopt their truths as your own. This is the hardest part of the shift; this is the final exam of sorts before promotion, and this is the test I've seen most people fail. Some people start doing well, but once loneliness pays them a visit, they return to the familial, platonic, romantic, professional, and ministerial relationships that God has delivered them from. They prioritize entertainment and man's acceptance over their assignment and God's acceptance. Then again, some people never stop idolizing their families, friends, lovers, pastors, organizations, and the like.

Understand that breaking up with your old heart is a

process, and it's typically not an overnight event. It took you years (decades even) to learn the toxic mindsets and ways that you've picked up, and it will take time to unlearn those lies and behaviors. And this is where the breakdown comes in. This is when we have to stop returning to our corpses and performing CPR on them. We have to let our old ways, old beliefs, and old mindsets decompose. To do this, we have to detach them from what we revere as valuable or invaluable. For example, let's say that you want to be married, and you are passionate about the idea of becoming someone's spouse. And you've attached this desire to a path; this path is the way you believe you must journey to get to this desire. So, you've reasoned within yourself that you have to eat healthy, exercise often, learn to cook a lot of dishes, and be seductive. This is what you were taught, and this is how most of your female predecessors managed to ensnare their husbands. And while your Uncle Earl may be still married to your Aunt Nancy, the truth is, the two of them have never succeeded in anything but remaining numbly married. In other words, they've learned to co-exist, tolerate one another, and wait for the Grim Reaper to see which one he chooses to take first. These principles could lead you to a husband, but they likely won't lead you to the right husband. Consequently, you may find yourself married to a man who is willing to tolerate you while entertaining other women. You have to be willing to throw all of what you once knew away, with the exception of God's Word, of course. You have to be willing to part ways with principles like:

- ✘ "Happy wife, happy life."
- ✘ "A man wants a woman who is a lady in the streets, but a freak between the sheets."

The first principle promotes witchcraft and control, whereas, the husband's happiness is predicated on whether or not he satisfies the needs, whelms, desires, and demands of his wife. It promotes the idea that he has to always be agreeable. And most of the older men who promote this principle chuckle nervously as their wives scour, purse their lips, roll their eyes, and proudly proclaim, "That's right!" Of course, some people who say this are just playfully echoing what they've heard others say, while some men are truly at the mercy of their wives, being abused and emasculated emotionally, verbally, and sometimes even physically. Yes, men suffer through abuse as well. While a husband should go out of his way to maintain a happy household, he still has the responsibility of leading that household, and sometimes, this means he has to say "no" to his wife. Sometimes, he has to say "yes" to her. The key is listening for the voice of the Holy Spirit, after all, while the husband is the head of the household, God loves to place wisdom in low places; this way, we have to humble ourselves to get it. For example, a husband can go weeks, months, and years trying to figure out the answer to a problem, and one day, he humbles himself and tells his wife about his issue. Within a matter of minutes, the wife he hid that problem from could solve it with a few words. The same is true for children. Sometimes, God can place the answer to your dilemma or your problems in the mouths of your children; this way, you have to humble yourself to get access to that wisdom. He can place wisdom in the mouth of a drug addict, a homeless person, someone suffering with mental illness, a deaf and dumb person, an alcoholic, an ex-lover or spouse or within the problem itself. No, you shouldn't seek this people out looking for wisdom, but when God leads you to a space or a place, go there. The answer to one of the most longstanding mysteries in your life can be solved by a simple act of obedience, coupled with humility.

Every ungodly mindset has to breakdown; this leads us to another level of "dying to ourselves," and it is the old you that has to die before you go out there, cut and dye your hair, and proudly introduce the world to what you proclaim to be the "new you." (Note: it's usually the old self wearing a costume and bound by more demonic principles). But to cause this breakdown, you have to continuously eat the Word and break it down; in other words, don't just memorize the scriptures and shout them out anytime you have a moment to showoff your knowledge bank. Take the Sword of Truth and slice away at every lie that serves to confuse you. This is how you vomit it out of your conscious mind and place a restraining order on it. The key is you must:

1. Breakdown the Word of God through in-depth Bible study.
2. Allow your flesh to breakdown as you deny and kill it by resisting every temptation that your old mind plays whenever you are alone with your thoughts. This sounds easy until those old habits

surface and wage war with you in your members.

3. Let the old self rot, but don't live with your corpse. In other words, don't allow guilt, shame, and condemnation to isolate and place a muzzle on you. Overcome the enemy with the blood of the Lamb and the word of your testimony (see Revelation 12:11).

And finally, you have to be willing to embrace the breakthrough. Most people would shout from the rooftops, "Oh yeah, that part would be easy," but it's often one of the hardest feats in this equation because we often tell ourselves that we shouldn't march into the Promised Land while our loved ones are still out in the wilderness pitching tents and going in cycles and circles. Take a lesson from Moses. You can't help them get free until you've learned to not only embrace your freedom, but to maintain it because every force that can test you will tempt you to return to what you once mastered —yes, the very mindsets, beliefs, and demons that once mastered you. Truth be told, many people return to their old ways because they deal with survivor's guilt, impostor's syndrome, and loneliness—all of which are strongholds of the mind. How is loneliness a stronghold? Because it's a lie. You are not alone; you are never alone. You only feel alone when you have created a habit of ignoring God, all the while idolizing people. And while it is not good for man to be alone, the truth is—God gives us everything and every relationship we need to fulfill our assignments in every given season, HOWEVER, we tend to have things that we want to accomplish, and sometimes, our plans involve people, namely people we know and/or prefer, and God does not partner with us outside of purpose. So, when we step outside of our proverbial Gardens of Eden or places of order, we step into the wilderness—a place of disorder and dysfunction. Dysfunction is the product of the human mind malfunctioning because it is being used outside of its design. And yes, it can and does get lonely in the wilderness; that is until the enemy sends a wild animal our way. That wild animal is typically a narcissist or a narcissistic person, because the wilderness is the place where God delivers us from idolatry, but if we forsake our deliverance to fulfill our desires, we then deliver ourselves to the clutches of the enemy through idolatry, rebellion, and witchcraft.

Embracing your breakthrough means to:

- Stop procrastinating as it relates to writing the book(s) God told you to write, fearing that someone from your past will read it, leading to you being persecuted and ostracized by your family. You can't serve them and God.

- Praying about and walking through the doors that God opens for you without overthinking or over-planning. You don't need to lose 45 more pounds, get a tummy tuck, and get breast implants before you turn the camera around and preach God's Word.

- Forgiving others daily. This doesn't mean that you have to give wayward people access to you, but you should have another grace every day to share with the people you've given access to you, as well as the people you come in contact with. You have to choose to forgive your assailant. Forgiveness is a choice, not a feeling. When you choose to forgive, how you feel about the individual changes, as well as their title in your mind. So, your assailant can easily become your assignment. Again, I can't emphasize this enough—this doesn't mean that you should reconnect with the individual or give them access to you; it does mean, on the other hand, that you should at least intercede for the individual. Sometimes, we come in contact with people, not because God wanted us to connect with them; instead, He allows us to meet them so that we can intercede for them.

- Getting the therapy and wise counsel you'll need to process what you've overcome and prepare you for what's to come.

- Shutting out every voice that attacks God's Word, your confidence, your self-esteem, or your identity. If someone keeps reminding you of who you were, that person's time in your life (at least on an intimate level) has expired. Ask God to place them where He wants them to be in your life, rather than where you want them to be.

- Reaping the benefits of your renewed mind without guilt or the need to share it with people who you feel a sense of obligation towards. Note: God won't enrich you if He knows you'll enrich people He's trying to save and deliver, thus making them comfortable in their wilderness seasons.

- Going back to school, starting the business, or doing whatever it is that God has given you the grace and the capability to do. Remember this—responsibility is how you respond to your abilities. If you respond properly, God will entrust you with more (see Luke 16:10). If you don't respond favorably, even what you have can and will be taken (see Matthew 13:12).

- Dislodging yourself from the concept of loyalty towards a person, and understanding that your loyalty belongs to God. To be loyal means to be faithful, and to be faithful means that your faith is full. It means to be consistent as a result of your faith. For example, a woman who is loyal to God in every dimension will, by default, be loyal to her husband. She doesn't become loyal or faithful to her husband; she is loyal and faithful to God which, in turn, makes her loyal to her husband. Loyalty to humans leads to idolatry, but loyalty to God leads to healthy marriages, relationships, partnerships, and the like, because in human relationships, individualism and opinions often get in the way. But when the Word is the foundation of any given relationship, both or all parties can unite by agreeing and complying with the Word.

- Growing and maturing consistently and intentionally. God doesn't want to give you a single breakthrough; He wants your life to be filled with breakthroughs, but you have to be willing to travel from one state of mind to another—repeatedly. To do this, you have to study the Word of God daily, apply the Word of God consistently, and promote God's Word every time you see an opportunity to do so.

- Sitting at tables where your ears have to put in more work than your mouth. What does this mean? When you sit at tables of familiarity, you aren't learning much; you're just sharing and entertaining one another. You may even be encouraging and edifying one another, and that's great! But growth can't happen if you're always teaching, preaching, and speaking. Growth happens when you listen and learn. This is why you have to sit at tables with people who are far wiser than you, along with people who are smarter than you, and get this—don't say something just to be a part of the conversation. Listen, learn, take notes, show honor, and pay the tab. If God is at that table, you want to be invited back to it. No worries. In due season, you'll have something to contribute to the conversation, but in the meantime, just show up early, be kind, and look like you belong at the table.

- Give God the glory repeatedly. Never steal God's glory from Him. One of the most common crimes that take place whenever we step into favor is the praise of man. People will celebrate you, flatter you, and even praise you. Give to God what belongs to Him. I'm not saying that you have to cut them off and religiously shout, "To God be the glory!" in an attempt to prove yourself to Heaven. No, we're dealing with legalities and principles. Your job is to make sure that whatever it is that you do points back to Him and not at you. You see, the praise of man is addictive, and it is one of the hardest addictions to overcome, especially if you are surrounded by the wrong people. Simply make God's name popular; for example, let's say that your book was to hit the bestseller's list. Don't boast about your intellect or yourself in any way. This will only encourage people to praise you. Instead, promote the book, but more than that, promote God. For example, don't say silly things like, "When I was a toddler, I knew I was special because I kept seeing baby angels, and when I was around 12, I discovered my unique ability to see demons." The word "idolatry" starts with "i." Instead, I would say, "God opened my eyes to see angels for as far back as I can remember, and when I was 12, He opened my eyes to see demons." In this, I'm keeping the primary focus of my testimony on Him, and not myself.

- Whatever you do, don't lose your gratitude! Don't become familiar with God's grace, His presence, or His blessings. What a believer lacks in gratitude, he or she will make up in pride and entitlement.

- Don't get too comfortable. Breakthrough is not a one-and-done event. I can break out of the prison cell, but I still have to break out of the prison, meaning, there are rooms and spaces I must go through to get to freedom. If I broke out of my cell and pitched a tent in the hallway, I'd be tossed into a stronger cell or, better yet, a greater stronghold.

As you can see, soul ties aren't what you thought they were. This is why a lot of believers have had trouble breaking them, but when we get the right information in our hands, we can then engage the spirit realm, demons, strongholds, and people in a more effective way. I recommend that you read this book several times so that you can transfer the information from your head to your heart, but definitely read your Bible more so you can measure the information in this book, as well as any other book you read with the Word of Truth.

Below, I've listed a few practical ways to break ungodly soul ties.

- Repent for the crimes you committed that got you in those soul ties in the first place.
- Get therapy.
- Get wise counsel, but only if you're teachable.
- Study the Word of God daily.
- Change your phone number.
- Get rid of the gifts your exes or anyone you were

soul-tied to (in an ungodly way) gave you; this includes letters, pictures, jewelry, teddy bears, perfume/cologne, etc. Only keep the children and the pets!

- Get rid of the items you sinned in and sinned on. I was ministering to a woman once who I used to speak with frequently over the phone. One day, she called me crying, saying that she'd fallen into the trap of masturbation. She hadn't masturbated in years, but that morning, she'd woken up feeling like she was on fire, so she gave in. The Lord had me to start talking about demonic attachments to clothing, items, and the like. Suddenly, she gasped. "Tiffany!" she shouted, cutting me off mid-sentence. "That's it!" The story went this way—she'd neglected to wash her clothes, so she didn't have any clean underwear. In desperation, she'd gone through her underwear drawer and found a pair of undies she used to wear when she was an exotic dancer (stripper). She'd put them on the night prior, and no, she hadn't worn those undergarments in years. That morning, she woke up battling with lust so much so that she'd been

tormented until she gave in and masturbated.
While talking with her, she told me that she was
heading to the kitchen to grab a garbage bag. She
then went through her house and threw a lot of
the items from her old lifestyle away. I'd
ministered these instructions to people for years,
and I've gotten some amazing feedback. If you
don't feel like this particular pointer is for you,
simply pray about it. Ask God to show you
everything in your life and in your home that He
wants you to throw away, and be prepared to obey
Him. Don't ignore Him once He responds.

- Delete your exes on social media (unless you have
children with them), and make it a point to not
stalk their profiles or the profiles of their lovers,
spouses, or the people you suspect they're seeing.
If this feat seems impossible, block them all until
you heal, and be sure to penalize yourself. For
example, give a certain amount of money to your
charity of choice every time you break the rule
you've set for yourself.

- Change the conversation. Tell your friends to stop
talking about your exes to you. To move forward,

you have to stop looking back.

- Set boundaries and enforce them. (Be sure to check out my Boundaries series, starting with the Black Book of Boundaries, the Green Book of Boundaries, the Blue Book of Boundaries, the Purple Book of Boundaries, and the Red Book of Boundaries) to learn how to masterfully set, solidify, and enforce boundaries.

- The return of the unclean spirit can and often does look like the return of an ex. Don't be flattered. Send the dude or the damsel to voicemail or, even better, block them or change your number.

- Create Godly and healthier habits. For example, for two years, I went on a date with God every Saturday as our Daddy/Daughter date. I would dress up, go to one of my favorite restaurants, dine in, and enjoy my food and my experience. I would then leave the restaurant and go do my weekly food/supply shopping. I remember God telling me to buy something for myself every week, even if it was something as small as a bottle of fingernail polish. In this, God was introducing me to Jehovah Jireh, the Lord who provides.

- Let God introduce every side of you to every side of Himself. This is how the lights turn on in every room.

- Change the channel. It is hard to break an ungodly soul tie when the music used to ensnare your soul is still playing in your ear. One golden rule I have is this—if it promotes sin or encourages me to sin against God, I won't listen to it. The same is true for movies. Stop following the crowd and rushing to see every demonic movie that hits the theaters. Keep your soul free from demonic contaminates. Over time, you'll notice a difference between yourself and the believers who watch and listen to anything that entertains them. You'll notice that you have peace, joy, and prosperity when they're wrestling with wounds that keep being reopened. You'll notice that you're more patient as well. As a matter of fact, when you don't have any weeds contending with the fruits of the Spirit in your life, you'll find that you'll have better harvests in less time.

- Stop dating people who remind you of your exes.

We are often attracted to a type, because our type is typically a spirit we've grown familiar with. If you're single, take yourself out of the dating arena and give that time and energy to God. Let Him deliver you from yourself; let Him reset your appetite, and let Him prepare you for marriage His way.

You can also adopt a pet (try your local kill shelters and save a life), take up new hobbies, travel the world, build businesses, and discover a life that you've never dreamed of having. You just have to be willing, and with that willingness, you have to move forward—now. Faith is always now; hope is always later. You move now, but you'll get there later, but if you wait now, you'll still be making excuses later. Planners plan; doers do. You are what you repeatedly do, so if you're always planning to do something, you're a planner. Howbeit, if you do what you're designed to do the moment you're empowered to do it, you'll become too blessed and busy to entertain ungodly soul ties. Remember, you got this because God's got you!

Severance & Deliverance Prayer

> If the Son therefore shall make you free, ye shall be free indeed.
>
> John 8:36

Let me make this one thing clear before we go any further. A soul tie is NOT a demon, therefore, it cannot be cast out. A soul tie isn't a rope that can be cut, nor is it a chain that can be broken. You can't say a few words, pray a special prayer, and poof, the soul tie is gone. It simply doesn't work like that. Remember, the soul is comprised of the mind, will, and emotions. The mind is what the Bible refers to as the heart. The heart is what God told us to guard (see Proverbs 4:23). There are several ways to guard the heart, and the Bible details them all.

- **2 Corinthians 10:5:** Casting down imaginations, and every high thing that exalteth itself against the knowledge of God, and bringing into captivity every thought to the obedience of Christ.
- **2 Corinthians 6:14:** Be ye not unequally yoked

together with unbelievers: for what fellowship hath righteousness with unrighteousness? and what communion hath light with darkness?

- **1 Corinthians 5:11:** But now I have written unto you not to keep company, if any man that is called a brother be a fornicator, or covetous, or an idolater, or a railer, or a drunkard, or an extortioner; with such an one no not to eat.
- **Proverbs 22:24:** Make no friendship with an angry man; and with a furious man thou shalt not go.
- **Romans 12:1:** I beseech you therefore, brethren, by the mercies of God, that ye present your bodies a living sacrifice, holy, acceptable unto God, which is your reasonable service.
- **1 Corinthians 15:33:** Be not deceived: evil communications corrupt good manners.
- **2 Corinthians 6:14:** Be ye not unequally yoked together with unbelievers: for what fellowship hath righteousness with unrighteousness? And what communion hath light with darkness?
- **Proverbs 13:20:** He that walketh with wise men shall be wise: but a companion of fools shall be

destroyed.

- **2 Thessalonians 3:6:** Now we command you, brethren, in the name of our Lord Jesus Christ, that ye withdraw yourselves from every brother that walketh disorderly, and not after the tradition which he received of us.

- **James 4:4:** Ye adulterers and adulteresses, know ye not that the friendship of the world is enmity with God? Whosoever therefore will be a friend of the world is the enemy of God.

Who you associate yourself with will determine who and what associates itself with you, both naturally and spiritually. Yes, this includes romantic partners. I mention this because, all too often, when the topic of association is brought up, most people only think about their friends. They don't consider their dealings with their family members or their romantic partners and what they subject themselves to. Consequently, some people have to repeatedly go through deliverance, not because of anything they're doing wrong, but because they have opened the door of their hearts to people who have opened their hearts to Satan. A general rule of thumb is this—never give anyone access to your heart who has trouble guarding their own. Think of it this way. You're married and faithful to your partner which, in a perfect world, should mean that you are never at risk for any sexually transmitted diseases. Howbeit, your partner isn't faithful, and because of his or her philandering ways, you are exposed to all manners of diseases, both curable and incurable. Is this fair to you? Absolutely not! So, why would you crucify your flesh every single day, denying yourself many of the pleasures this world has to offer, only to be ensnared by your best friend's demons simply because she doesn't fear God and wants to live on the wild side? While you're at home reading your Bible, she's out in the streets picking up demons, and now those demons have access to you through her. Being unequally yoked with unbelievers goes way beyond you soul-tying yourself to a non-Christian, it also involves illegally connecting yourself to someone who identifies as a Christian but does not bear the fruits of the Spirit. Please understand that the church at large is jam-packed with both tares and wheat. Matthew 7:21 reads, "Not every one that saith unto me, Lord, Lord, shall enter into the kingdom of heaven; but

he that doeth the will of my Father which is in heaven."
How do you differentiate tares from wheat? Matthew
7:16-20 answers this question eloquently; it reads, "Ye
shall know them by their fruits. Do men gather grapes of
thorns, or figs of thistles? Even so every good tree
bringeth forth good fruit; but a corrupt tree bringeth
forth evil fruit. A good tree cannot bring forth evil
fruit, neither *can* a corrupt tree bring forth good
fruit. Every tree that bringeth not forth good fruit is
hewn down, and cast into the fire. Wherefore by their
fruits ye shall know them." But wait! What does this
mean? Simply put, your job is to examine their lives and
words (for out of the abundance of the heart, the mouth
speaks) to see what fruits they produce. Do you see the
fruits of the Spirit continuously growing and bearing
fruit in their lives, or do you repeatedly see the works of
the flesh at work in their lives? As a reminder, here are
the charts below.

Fruit of the Spirit		
Love	Joy	Peace
Patience	Kindness	Goodness
Faithfulness	Gentleness	Self Control

Works of the Flesh		
Adultery	Fornication	Uncleanness
Lasciviousness	Idolatry	Witchcraft
Hatred	Variance	Emulations
Wrath	Strife	Seditions
Heresies	Envyings	Murders
Drunkenness		Revelings

But this isn't just it! Because a LOT of people will testify that they've dated and married folks they've met in the church who appeared to have many fruits of the Spirit, and did not appear to be "bad people," and they ended up being narcissistic, toxic, demonized souls with a penchant for evil. Were they deceived? Yep, but not by the narcissist himself or herself. They were deceived by their own sinful desires. James 1:14 confirms this; it reads, "But every man is tempted, when he is drawn away of his own lust, and enticed." So, before we can do an external fruit inspection on another person, we have to regain our ability to see clearly by inspecting and cleaning up our own hearts. Matthew 7:1-3 states, "Judge not, that ye be not judged. For with what judgment ye judge, ye shall be judged: and with what measure ye mete, it shall be measured to you again. And why beholdest thou the mote that is in thy brother's eye, but considerest not the beam that is in thine own eye?" This scripture is often taken out of context by lukewarm believers who love their sins more than they love the Word of God. God is not telling us to look away and never judge another believer; this is a scripture against hypocrisy! For example, how can you rebuke the man at church who's involved in a same-sex relationship when you are in fornication? Same crime, different partners. In this, God is saying to clean up your heart so that you can effectively help someone else to get free. This is to say—a believer who is, will be, or has been deceived by another "believer" is not faultless. Deception has to have something to stick itself to, and as mentioned earlier, it sticks to ungodly desires; it also sticks to impatience, double-mindedness, faithless religion, fear, doubt, idolatry, rebellion, and the list goes on. This is why God told us in Matthew 6:33, "But seek ye first the kingdom of God, and his righteousness; and all these things shall be added unto you." The cure for idolatry is seeking God FIRST! This doesn't mean that you first become a Christian, and then you can do what you want safely. Even after getting saved, you have to seek God while He can be found (see Isaiah 55:6). What this means is—God will avail Himself to us for oh-so-long before He turns us over to a reprobate mind; that is if we don't want Him enough to seek Him, but instead, seek to fulfill the desires of our own wicked hearts. The word "first" deals with chronology obviously; it deals with order, protocol, and proper arrangement. Whatever you seek first becomes your head, and the head represents the authority over your life. If you seek anything or anyone, including your own selfish desires and plans over God, you will pick up a head or authority called idolatry, and that issue will invite in a sleuth of demons, the most pronounced ones being Jezebel and Leviathan. They'll either come in and become tenants in your soul or they'll come to you in physical form. This simply means that you will meet and likely partner yourself with demonized people who are bound by those spirits, and those people will begin to rule over you either covertly or overtly. Either way, you might be a citizen of Heaven, but you'd also be an occupant of hell on Earth. I said all of this to simply say—yes, I will publish a prayer to help you stretch and strain the soul ties that you have, BUT those ties will only break when you come out of agreement with the sins you're in or the sins you were in. The prayer below can fully sever ungodly soul ties if you give up your ungodly ways. In short, you can't be delivered from your soul tie with Jason if you're not willing to repent for fornication because the tie that links the two of you is rebellion! A soul tie is NOT an invisible string that can be prayed away; it is agreement! Amos 3:3 says, "Can two walk together, except they be agreed?" The tie itself is agreement! I remember when the Lord told me to let go of an old friend of mine, and I didn't know what this process would look like. I thought He wanted me to call her over the phone and announce to her that I could no longer be her friend. This felt like an impossibility for me at the time because we'd be friends for well over two decades. So, I did what any sensible person would do—I prayed about it. I told God how I felt and asked Him for direction. He simplified it for me. He wasn't telling me to call her on the phone and read some platonic form of a Dear John letter. He was simply telling me to change my mind! What connected me to my old friend was a group of principles we were both in agreement with! There were some things I had to get delivered from—there were some old thinking patterns I had to do away with, and by studying the Word and applying it, I would simultaneously be severing the tie between me and my former friend because we would no longer be in agreement. She wasn't bad. We were just unequally yoked; she knew who I once was, but she had trouble embracing who I'd become and who I was growing into, and that's the real Tiffany. This is to say that soul ties are broken when we break up with the lies of the enemy, allow God to plant the Word in our hearts, and then allow the Word to bear fruits in our lives. This fruit, once it emerges, is what we call breakthrough. So, there has to be a breakup before there is a breakdown, and there has to be a breaking down of old principles in order for there to be a breakthrough. So, before you say the prayer below, repent. Only you and God know everything that you need to repent for, and remember, repentance isn't just an "I'm sorry" ceremony followed by tears and tongues. Repentance means to turn around, to change your ways, to come out of sin, and to come out of agreement with the enemy of your soul. I'm sharing this because I don't want to deceive you into thinking that saying a specialized prayer and having a cry session will make those thoughts of Willie go away. They won't. You have to come out of agreement with the principles and the plans you had with Willie. You have to fight for your mind; you have to place your mind back on Christ and leave it there. You have to agree with God's Word; that's it and that's all. And note that after the prayer, you may still have to grieve the relationship, block the individual on social media, change your phone number, penalize yourself anytime you look the individual up on social media, cut ties with his or her family, and find something else to do with your time. Obviously, the best and the most effective way to invest your time is by studying the Bible, praying, and through a daily application of the Word in your life. But without further adieu, here's the prayer:

> Lord, I repent for my sins, both known and
> unknown. I repent for not adhering to your Word
> in my life and in my relationships. I repent for
> sexual sin, bad association, trauma bonds, and
> every ungodly soul tie I've bound myself with. I
> come out of agreement with sexual sin, bad

association, and anything that has given the enemy a legal right in my life. Lord, you said in 1 John 1:9 that if we confess our sins, you are faithful and just to forgive us our sins, and to cleanse us from all unrighteousness. Lord, I confess to you (use this time to confess your sins to the Lord), and I renounce and repent of those sins, in the name of Christ Jesus. I thank you for your grace and mercy, and I ask that you set me free today from the demons, strongholds, and the issues that came into my heart, body, and life as a result of those sins, in Jesus' name. Amen.

You're not done just yet. Next, please repeat the following proclamation:

I come out of agreement with every lie, scheme, and plan of the enemy right now, and I bind every unclean spirit that has entered my body, my soul, or my life as a result of my sins. I don't want you; you have no legal right to occupy space in my body, mind, or soul, so I command you in the name of Jesus Christ, to come up and out of me now! I sever every ungodly soul tie, yoke, chain, or bond that is holding me captive, and I command those ties to break right now, in Jesus' name! I decree and declare that, I am free because the Son has set me free, and I command any and every spirit that would rise up against my freedom to go into the abyss right now! I decree and declare that you must remain in the abyss until you're cast into the lake of fire by the Most High God! Devil, you can no longer operate in my life. I claim the blood of Jesus as my inheritance, and I have a legal right to freedom! Everything that is unlike God, leave me now, in Jesus' name! I release myself from shame, guilt, and condemnation, and I decree that I am more than a conqueror in Christ Jesus! Amen!

Remember, freedom can be permanent or it can be temporary; it all depends on how you respond to temptation and negative stimuli from here on out. How did Jesus respond to the woman caught in the sin of adultery? He told her to go away and sin no more. He still lives and He still speaks, and that's His declaration to all of us—go away and sin no more! Please keep in mind that sin is more than the act of fornication or the act of anger; it is always a lack of faith—ALWAYS! When we lack faith, the iniquity in us produces the works of the flesh (including fornication and anger), but when we have faith, we then receive the benefits of righteousness (availed to us through the death and resurrection of Christ). It's not by your works that you'll be made righteous; it's by your faith, and your faith will always show up in your works! What you do will change when you have a change of heart.

> Yea, a man may say, Thou hast faith, and I have works: shew me thy faith without thy works, and I will shew thee my faith by my works.
> James 2:18

9 781955 557603